PRAY LIKE A PROPHET

MARY DONNA HANKLA

Book Cover by Lou Designs @lgr202

Illustrations by Katerina R @katerinars

1st edition 2024

ISBN: 979-8-9880394-6-4

Library of Congress Control Number: 2024916796

All Scriptures used are from THE HOLY BIBLE, NEW INTERNATIONAL VERSION®, NIV® Copyright © 1973, 1978, 1984, 2011 by Biblica, Inc.™

CONTENTS

Dedication vii

Foreword...ix

Introduction: The Power of Prophetic Prayer xi

Chapter 1   Elijah - Revival and Leadership..............1
Chapter 2   Moses - Guidance and Deliverance......17
Chapter 3   Amos - Justice and Righteousness........33
Chapter 4   Isaiah - Vision and Hope 51
Chapter 5   Jeremiah - Perseverance and
             Restoration 67
Chapter 6   Ezekiel - Renewal and Rebirth.............85
Chapter 7   Daniel - Wisdom and Protection 109
Chapter 8   Hosea - Love and Redemption...........129
Chapter 9   Jonah - Obedience and Mercy 145
Chapter 10   Malachi - Faithfulness and Covenant 161
Chapter 11   Women Prophets 177
Chapter 12   The Unknown Prophets....................189

Conclusion: Embracing the Power of
      Prophetic Prayer 199

DEDICATION

I am grateful for all the people God has brought into my life to encourage me to seek the Scriptures. When I was a teenager, Larry and Kay Smith were my 4-H leaders. In addition to teaching us about 4-H, they taught us the Bible. Those Bible stories really inspired me!

I dedicate this book to my husband, Kenneth Hankla, and my son, Chris Hankla. Both have stood by me in this pursuit to write. Kenny provides encouragement, while Chris is the glue that brings the book together. Chris also provides technical support and reassures a successful book launch! Chris has spent countless hours to assure that the book is published with excellence.

I express gratitude for all who support me in prayer, with much thanks to Ron and Sandra Fowler for their constant encouragement. Also, I appreciate my prayer partner, Libby Repass.

Much appreciation is expressed to Katrina Sheffield, my niece, a faithful follower!

Johanna Cantrell, has gone to heaven. She was a faithful prayer partner, very active in prophecy.

Finally, I acknowledge the Women's Aglow organization. They taught me much about prophecy, and prayer. Jane Young, has now gone on to be with the Lord. She taught me to blow the shofar, and to pray over regions. With her, prayer for 7 East Coast States was offered.

FOREWORD

Pastor Lacy Griffith and his lovely wife, Goldie, wrote a beautiful Foreword. This pastor has greatly inspired me in the area of prayer. Pastor Lacy has faith that stands against all odds. Even in his older years, he serves God with great passion and prays with zeal.

My name is Pastor Lacy Griffith, Pastor of Yukon Pentecostal Holiness Church in West Virginia. I have pastored for 62 years. Several years ago, I led community prayer services once a month for the McDowell County. Pastor Donna Hankla assisted me with many of these meetings. During these prayer meetings for the County, God's Presence moved in powerful ways.

I highly recommend Mary Donna Hankla's new book, "Praying Like A Prophet." This book reviews a number of different prophets and their approaches to prayer. When these prophets prayed, mighty miracles happened. We can also pray with great power.

Pastor Hankla has been a friend for many years. She sets an excellent example for prayer with everyone she comes in contact with. I am honored to be her friend.

I would suggest that people read all of her books, and grow in the area of prayer.

I have also preached in West Virgina churches for 62 years, throughout the county and the state. I strongly believe in prayer, and I know that God will answer in His time.

Mary Donna Hankla is a great prayer warrior, and also Pastor of the Big Four Pentecostal Holiness Church in Kimball, WV. She lives what she teaches and preaches.

My parents were Pastor Jack and Lena Griffith. They set an example of prayer in our home. They encouraged me to pursue the ministry. At the age of five, in our neighborhood, I was called the "fence line preacher." This is because I walked around with my little Bible and preached to the chickens.

The Holy Spirit is poured out upon us as we pray. God's Spirit enables us to pursue prayer with great discipline.

We all have stories to tell. I am sure Mary Donna Hankla could fill many books with these inspired stories. I enjoy reading all that she publishes and am looking for many more to come.

God Bless All!

Pastor Lacy Griffith
War, WV

THE POWER OF PROPHETIC PRAYER

Prayer is our way of connecting with God. Prophetic prayer takes this connection even deeper. Prophetic prayer goes deeper than asking God for what we need. It's about standing with God, hearing His plans, and speaking His will into our lives, families, communities, and nations. This type of prayer helped Elijah call down fire from heaven, guided Moses to free his people, and gave Daniel courage in the lion's den. Prophetic prayer can bring revival, justice, hope, and God's miracles.

Think about what could happen if we used this powerful prayer in our own lives. By learning from the prophets, we can use the same power they did to do amazing things for God. When we pray prophetically, we align our hearts with God's heart. His Spirit guides our words and actions. This deepens our relationship with God and makes us His instruments, able to influence the world with His truth and love. Prophetic prayer invites us to go beyond the ordinary and step into the extraordinary. It calls us to be active in God's work on earth.

Welcome to "Pray Like a Prophet: Guiding Your Nation, City, Home, Family, and Self Through the Wisdom of the Prophets." In this book, we'll explore the lives and messages of the Bible's most powerful voices, the prophets, to uncover the truth of prophetic prayer and its transformative power.

UNDERSTANDING THE CALL

Prophetic prayer is a profound spiritual practice that connects us with God's heart and His divine purposes. The prophets we'll explore—Elijah, Moses, Amos, Isaiah, Jeremiah, Ezekiel, Daniel, Hosea, Jonah, and Malachi—were ordinary people called to communicate God's extraordinary messages. Their prayers were powerful declarations aligned with God's will, bringing revival, guidance, justice, hope, perseverance, renewal, wisdom, love, and faithfulness.

These prophetic prayers were anchored in a deep relationship with God and an unwavering faith in His promises. By understanding and emulating their approach to prayer, we can experience similar transformative power in our own lives.

THE IMPORTANCE OF PROPHETIC PRAYER

Prophetic prayer is essential for us as believers because it impacts every aspect of our lives—our personal relationship with God, our families, our communities, and even our nations. The prophets' prayers were intertwined with their mission to guide, correct, and uplift the people around them. Their prayers were acts of faith, expressions of obedience, and instruments of divine intervention.

Through this book, you will see how prophetic prayer can:

- Bring about national and community revival, just as Elijah's prayers brought rain and ended a drought.

- Provide guidance and deliverance in our personal and collective journeys, as seen in Moses' leadership of the Israelites.

- Advocate for justice and righteousness in our society, following Amos' example of speaking out against injustice.

- Sustain hope and vision in challenging times, inspired by Isaiah's prophecies of redemption.

- Encourage perseverance through trials and trust in God's restoration, demonstrated by Jeremiah's endurance.

- Foster spiritual renewal and rebirth, echoing Ezekiel's visions of dry bones coming to life.

- Grant divine wisdom and protection, exemplified by Daniel's life in exile.

- Reflect God's love and redemption in our relationships, inspired by Hosea's story of unrelenting love.

- Embrace obedience and extend mercy, as Jonah learned in his mission to Nineveh.

- Cultivate faithfulness and honor our covenant with God, following Malachi's call to return to sincere worship.

PURPOSE OF THIS BOOK

The purpose of "Pray Like a Prophet" is to inspire and equip you to incorporate prophetic prayer into your daily life. Each chapter explores the life of a prophet, exploring the unique lessons they offer and how their prayers can guide us today. By understanding their struggles, triumphs, and the context of their ministries, we can better align our own prayers with God's will.

This book will deepen your understanding of prophetic prayer, providing practical tools to enhance your prayer life. Whether praying for personal issues, family matters, community concerns, or national challenges, the prophets' examples will help you pray with boldness, faith, and a heart aligned with God's purposes.

EMBRACING THE JOURNEY

As you embark on this journey through the lives of the prophets, I encourage you to open your heart to their lessons and insights. Allow their stories to inspire and challenge you. Reflect on their prayers and consider how you can integrate their principles into your own prayer life.

This journey is about experiencing the transformative power of prophetic prayer in your own life. By walking in the footsteps of these remarkable ambassadors of the Lord, you will deepen your relationship with God, enrich your prayer life, and ignite a passion for His purposes in your life and the world around you.

Welcome to "Pray Like a Prophet." Together, let us embrace the wisdom of the prophets and the power of prophetic prayer to transform our lives and the lives of those around us.

1

ELIJAH - REVIVAL AND LEADERSHIP

In the bustling heart of a divided nation, where the whispers of false gods clashed against the memory of the one true God, there arose a man whose name would forever be etched in God's Word. His name was Elijah, a prophet of profound boldness and unwavering faith, chosen to lead his people back to the light of God.

To truly grasp Elijah's story, we must look at the times in which he lived. The people of Israel, God's chosen ones, had turned their backs on Him, succumbing to the allure of Baal and other false idols. It was in this time of spiritual drought that Elijah emerged, a voice of hope and truth. His mission was clear: to call the nation back to God, to ignite a revival that would restore faith and righteousness.

Elijah's story is a testament to what one person, wholly devoted to God, can accomplish. He stood before kings and commoners alike, unyielding in his message that the Lord alone is God. His boldness was not born out of arrogance but from an intimate knowledge of God's power and a burning desire to see His people return to Him.

BOLDNESS AND FAITH

Elijah's life teaches us about boldness and faith. He stood on Mount Carmel, facing the prophets of Baal. The odds seemed insurmountable, but Elijah knew that with God, the impossible becomes possible: *"Then you call on the name of your god, and I will call on the name of the Lord. The god who answers by fire—he is God"* (1 Kings 18:24). His faith was more than a private conviction; it was a public declaration. He didn't whisper his prayers; he shouted them, confident that God would respond.

In our own lives, we often face situations that seem overwhelming. Whether it's a personal crisis, a family issue, or a broader societal challenge, Elijah's example encourages us to step out in bold faith. We must remember that our boldness in prayer and action is rooted in our faith in God's power. Elijah teaches us to pray big prayers, to ask for the miraculous, and to expect God to move in mighty ways: *"Now to him who is able to do immeasurably more than all we ask or imagine, according to his power that is at work within us"* (Ephesians 3:20).

PRAYING FOR LEADERS

Elijah's story is a clarion call for us to pray for national revival and leadership. Look around at the state of our world. Division, moral decay, and spiritual apathy are rampant. But just as Elijah prayed for rain and saw a cloud the size of a man's hand, we too can pray for a spiritual outpouring. *"If my people, who are called by my name, will humble themselves and pray and seek my face and turn from their wicked ways, then I will hear from heaven, and I will forgive their sin and will heal their land"* (2 Chronicles 7:14).

Praying for our leaders is a commandment from God Himself. Elijah's interactions with King Ahab show us the importance of speaking truth to power and praying for those in authority. Imagine the courage it took for Elijah to confront Ahab, the most powerful man in the land, and declare that his actions were leading the nation astray. This was not a comfortable or safe mission, but Elijah's faith in God's word gave him the strength to stand firm. *"For lack of guidance a nation falls, but victory is won through many advisers"* (Proverbs 11:14).

Ask God to grant our leaders wisdom to make decisions that honor Him and benefit the people. Pray that our leaders will lead with integrity, resisting corruption and self-interest. Pray that our leaders will have the courage to stand for what is right, even when it's unpopular.

Our prayers must align with Scripture, ensuring they are in harmony with God's will. Elijah's prayers were powerful because they were based on God's promises and commands.

PERSISTENCE IN PRAYER

One of the most profound moments in Elijah's ministry was his prayer for rain. After a long drought, he prayed fervently, sending his servant to look toward the sea seven times. On the seventh time, the servant saw a small cloud, and Elijah knew that God had answered. *"And Elijah said to Ahab, 'Go, eat and drink, for there is the sound of a heavy rain.' So Ahab went off to eat and drink, but Elijah climbed to the top of Carmel, bent down to the ground and put his face between his knees"* (1 Kings 18:41-42). This story reminds us of the importance of persistence in prayer. Sometimes, we may not see immediate results, but like Elijah, we must keep praying, trusting that God hears us and will answer in His perfect timing.

When you pray for revival and leadership, don't be discouraged if change doesn't happen overnight. *Keep praying, keep believing,* and *keep looking* for that small cloud, the first sign that God is moving.

OBEDIENCE AND HOPE

Elijah's life is also a testament to the power of obedience. When God called him to confront Ahab, he didn't hesitate. When God instructed him to go to the widow at Zarephath, he went. And when God told him to return to Ahab and prophesy rain, he obeyed without question. This unwavering obedience is what set Elijah apart and allowed him to be used mightily by God. *"So he did what the Lord had told him"* (1 Kings 17:5).

Obedience is often the hardest part of our walk with God. It's easy to pray and ask for things, but it's much harder to step out in faith and do what God has called us to do, especially when it seems impossible or illogical. Yet, it's in those moments of obedience that God's power is most clearly revealed.

Elijah's obedience teaches us that God's plans are always better than our own, and His timing is always perfect.

The story of Elijah is a story of hope. It's a reminder that no matter how far we've strayed, no matter how deep the darkness seems, God is always there, ready to bring us back to Him. He is a God of second chances, a God who can bring life out of death, hope out of despair, and revival out of ruins. *"For I know the plans I have for you,"* declares the Lord, *"plans to prosper you and not to harm you, plans to give you hope and a future"* (Jeremiah 29:11).

As we face the challenges of our own time, let us draw strength from Elijah's example. Let us be bold in our faith, persistent in our prayers, and unwavering in our obedience. Let us trust that the same God who answered Elijah's prayers and brought revival to Israel can do the same in our lives and in our world today.

Take a moment now to think about the areas in your life where you need revival. Where do you need God's intervention? What are the dry, barren places that need the rain of His Spirit? Write them down and commit to praying for them daily, just as Elijah prayed for rain. Believe that God can and will bring renewal and restoration.

ELIJAH PRAYING FOR RAIN

The story of Elijah praying for rain is a powerful testament to persistent faith and the miraculous provision of God. Following a prolonged drought in Israel, Elijah engaged in fervent prayer for rain, demonstrating unwavering faith in God's promise to end the drought.

After a significant confrontation with the prophets of Baal on Mount Carmel, where God showed His supremacy by consuming Elijah's sacrifice with fire from heaven, Elijah turned his attention to praying for rain. He climbed to the top of Mount Carmel, bent down to the ground, and put his face between his knees—a posture of intense prayer and humility before God.

"Go and look toward the sea," he told his servant. The servant went and looked, but returned with a report that there was nothing. Elijah sent him back seven times, each time persisting in prayer despite the servant's repeated reports of no change. On the seventh time, the servant came back with a different message: *"A cloud as small as a man's hand is rising from the sea"* (1 Kings 18:44).

This tiny cloud, seemingly insignificant in size, was a sign of the impending answer to Elijah's prayer. Elijah's faith saw beyond the small beginnings, recognizing it as the precursor to the abundant rain God had promised. He instructed his servant to tell King Ahab to prepare his chariot and go down before the rain stopped him.

Soon, the sky grew black with clouds, the wind rose, and a heavy rain began to fall, ending the drought and demonstrating God's faithfulness and power. Elijah's persistence in prayer, even when there were no immediate signs of change, teaches us about the importance of faith and perseverance. His story encourages us to continue praying and trusting in God's promises, even when the evidence of His answers seems small or delayed. The cloud, though small at first, was the harbinger of a great downpour, symbolizing how God often starts His miracles in seemingly insignificant ways.

THE LEGACY OF ELIJAH

Elijah's story is a powerful reminder that prayer is not just a spiritual discipline, but a mighty weapon that brings about change in our lives and in our world. It has the power to change hearts, transform lives, and alter the course of nations. Let us commit to being people of prayer, following the example of Elijah, and believing that God can do the impossible. *"The prayer of a righteous person is powerful and effective"* (James 5:16).

Elijah's life challenges us to think bigger, pray bolder, and believe that God can do more than we could ever ask or imagine. His story is a testament to the fact that one person, fully surrendered to God, can make an extraordinary difference. It's a call to each of us to step out in faith, to be bold in our prayers, and to trust that God is still in the business of miracles.

So, as you reflect on the life of Elijah, let his story inspire you to live with the same kind of boldness and faith. Let it encourage you to pray with confidence, to believe in the impossible, and to trust in the God who can bring revival to our lives, our communities, and our nation.

MARCHING SPIRIT ARMIES

With great joy Mary Donna Hankla shares encounters with God that inspired her to become an intercessor for the nation. At the age of 17, she began experiencing prophetic words and scenes from the Holy Spirit. Every experience has been confirmed by the golden standard, God's Word!

The fight for her family was the first heavenly order. Her family instilled values of diligence, dedication and hard work. Many summers were spent working on the farm, tending crops such as tobacco, beans, strawberries, and squash. These crops provided money for college education. The entire family believed in the importance of good jobs.

However, the family experienced great struggles during her teen-age years. These struggles brought Donna to Bible Study groups held before the start of school. God's Spirit moved powerfully during the study and prayer sessions. And when Donna welcomed The Holy Spirit into her life, supernatural encounters brought great strength and assurance. Donna prayed and fasted often for the family. And today, every family member serves God in some capacity.

Stepping stones of intercession presented themselves to Donna, and brought her to Washington, D.C., for several years on the National Day of Prayer. Donna and a team from the Appalachian Conference of the IPHC were invited to participate in this yearly event. At these national prayer events, God's Presence swept through the room, and touched the hearts of the intercessors.

THE ENCOUNTER WITH THE SPIRIT ARMIES

I lived in a room with two other girls at Emory & Henry College, Emory, Viriginia. All of us shared a deep belief in the power of prayer, and we attended Bible Study groups.

After supper, one autumn evening, I was delighted to feel refreshing bursts of wind blowing into the room from an open window. Soon, the evening would turn into the dark of the night. I took a break from exhausting study sessions for an Anatomy Test the following day. I looked out the window, and saw vibrant colors of fall all around us. The college campus was surrounded by hills which were dotted with numerous trees. The leaves had turned into brilliant colors of yellow and red.

Soon, I laid down and dozed off to sleep. My eyes had become heavy with sleep. But I would not sleep very long. A luminous light lit up the entire room. And the light switch was turned off! The other girls sat up in their beds. We realized that God's Presence was in our midst, so we began to pray. After about an hour, it became evident that this would be an all-night visit.

We sensed in our spirits, that we should stay awake and pray, and wait in the Presence of the Lord. We all knew that we should stay alert. We were about to experience an encounter that would last a lifetime. For indeed, one of the girls became a Methodist minister. I obtained

Bachelor's and Master's degrees in education. Also, I became an ordained minister, and a prayer leader.

Suddenly, I heard LOUD marching. It was so loud that I was drawn to the window to see what was happening. I thought that the cadets were practicing. There was a Marching Army, but it was not of this world. Spirits were marching! I could tell that they were following a Spirit General. They marched right by my window. They marched in a cadence. Spirit after spirit just kept coming. It seemed that they marched for at least 30 minutes!

I wanted to know what was happening. So, I asked the Lord about this marching army.

And I sensed that the Holy Spirit gave the following response.

"This is the army of the Lord. You will join this army in due time. It will be an army of intercessors. You will meet many prayer warriors."

"They charge like warriors;
 they scale walls like soldiers.
They all march in line,
 not swerving from their course." (Joel 2:7)

Shortly, after midnight, we all fell asleep. But we would not sleep long. This was a night for us to wait in God's

Presence. And God's Spirit would help us keep this Prayer Watch!

The room began to shake so violently that the beds literally moved a few feet! No sleep for us. This heavenly encounter was of greater value than sleep!

After this encounter with the Marching Spirits, I became more zealous to pursue a life of prayer, and become a leader of prayer on several different levels.

REFLECTION QUESTIONS

1. Reflecting on Elijah's boldness in standing up against the prophets of Baal, when was the last time you demonstrated bold faith in a challenging situation? How did it impact your relationship with God and others around you?

2. Elijah prayed persistently for rain despite not seeing immediate results. Are there areas in your life where you have become discouraged and stopped praying? How can Elijah's example inspire you to persist in prayer?

3. Elijah obeyed God's instructions even when they seemed difficult. Are there areas in your life where you feel God is calling you to step out in faith and obedience? What is holding you back, and how can you overcome those obstacles?

4. Consider the importance of praying for leaders as highlighted in Elijah's story. Who are the leaders in your community or nation that you can commit to praying for regularly? What specific qualities (wisdom, integrity, courage) will you pray for them to possess?

5. Reflect on the need for spiritual revival in your own life and community. What specific areas in

your life need God's intervention and renewal? How can you actively seek and pray for revival in those areas, drawing inspiration from Elijah's faith and persistence?

Prayer

Lord, thank You for the powerful example of Elijah. Help us to live with the same kind of boldness and faith. Teach us to pray with confidence, to believe in the impossible, and to trust in Your mighty power. Bring revival to our hearts, our homes, and our nation. In Jesus' name, Amen.

2

MOSES - GUIDANCE AND DELIVERANCE

In the story of God's chosen people, no figure looms larger than Moses. His journey from the palaces of Egypt to the wilderness of Sinai, leading the Israelites to freedom, is one of the most compelling stories in the Bible. Moses' life embodies the themes of guidance and deliverance, offering us profound lessons on trusting in God's promises and seeking His direction in our own lives.

Born into a time of intense persecution, Moses' life began with a desperate act of faith. His mother, Jochebed, placed him in a basket among the reeds of the Nile to save him from Pharaoh's decree to kill all Hebrew male infants. This act of faith was the beginning of Moses' journey—a journey marked by God's providence and guidance.

Raised in the Egyptian royal household, Moses was educated and groomed for leadership, yet his Hebrew heritage could not be ignored. After killing an Egyptian for beating a Hebrew slave, Moses fled to Midian, where he lived as a shepherd. It was here, in the solitude of the wilderness, that God called him from the burning bush, commissioning him to lead the Israelites out of bondage. *"So now, go. I am sending you to Pharaoh to bring my people the Israelites out of Egypt" (Exodus 3:10).* This divine mandate was daunting, yet Moses' journey illustrates the power of trusting in God's promises, even when the path seems impossible.

Moses' initial response to God's call was one of hesitation and doubt. He questioned his own abilities and the likelihood of success. *"Who am I that I should go to Pharaoh and bring the Israelites out of Egypt?"* (Exodus 3:11). Yet, God assured him, *"I will be with you"* (Exodus 3:12). This promise was the foundation of Moses' mission. Throughout the plagues, the Exodus, and the wandering in the desert, Moses' leadership was continually tested. The crossing of the Red Sea stands as a monumental testament to God's deliverance. When the Israelites found themselves trapped between Pharaoh's advancing army and the sea, Moses trusted in God's command: *"Raise your staff and stretch out your hand over the sea to divide the water so that the Israelites can go through the sea on dry ground"* (Exodus 14:16). This act of faith resulted in a miraculous deliverance, cementing Moses' role as the leader chosen by God.

In our own lives, we often face "Red Sea moments"—times when we feel trapped and see no way out. Moses' story reminds us that trusting in God's promises can lead to miraculous deliverance. Moses' relationship with God was intimate and direct. He often sought God's guidance through prayer and communion, which is a powerful model for us. The name that God revealed to Moses, *"I AM WHO I AM"* (Exodus 3:14), signifies His eternal presence and unchanging nature. This name reassures us that the same God who guided Moses is with us today, ready to lead us through our own challenges.

When facing difficult decisions or uncertain paths, we can call upon THE GREAT I AM for guidance. Our prayers should reflect our dependence on God's wisdom and direction. To seek God's guidance in our daily lives, we must cultivate a habit of prayer and scripture meditation. Start each day with a prayer for guidance. Acknowledge God's sovereignty and ask for His direction in every decision you face. Immerse yourself in God's Word. The Bible is filled with guidance and wisdom that can illuminate your path. After praying, spend time in silence, listening for God's voice. Sometimes guidance comes through a still, small voice. Write down your prayers, thoughts, and any impressions you receive. This helps to clarify your thoughts and recognize patterns in God's guidance. Seek counsel from godly mentors and friends. *"For lack of guidance a nation falls, but victory is won through many advisers"* (Proverbs 11:14). God often speaks through the wisdom of others.

The Bible is filled with stories of divine guidance. Apart from Moses, we see God's leading in the lives of many others. Abraham was called to leave his homeland and go to a place God would show him (Genesis 12:1). David was anointed as King over Israel (2 Samuel 5:4).

God's Spirit gave him great victories in many battles. Also, he overcame many leadership challenges.

Prophetic prayer is about aligning our hearts and minds with God's will. When we pray for guidance, we acknowledge that God's wisdom far surpasses our own. Reflect on areas in your life where you need God's guidance. Are there decisions or challenges that seem overwhelming? Write them down and commit to seeking God's direction through prayer, scripture, and the counsel of trusted believers.

Moses' journey was not just about guidance but also about deliverance. The story of the Exodus is a powerful reminder of God's ability to rescue His people from bondage and oppression. The Passover, the final plague, was a profound act of deliverance. God instructed the Israelites to mark their doorposts with the blood of a lamb, and the angel of death passed over their homes. This event prefigured the ultimate deliverance through Jesus Christ, the Lamb of God. *"The blood will be a sign for you on the houses where you are, and when I see the blood, I will pass over you. No destructive plague will touch you when I strike Egypt" (Exodus 12:13).*

This deliverance from Egypt was a physical manifestation of God's saving power, but it also pointed to the spiritual deliverance that Jesus would bring.

Just as God delivered the Israelites from physical bondage, He delivers us from spiritual bondage. Sin, fear, and despair can hold us captive, but through Christ, we have the promise of freedom. *"It is for freedom that Christ has set us free"* (Galatians 5:1). Reflect on areas in your life where you need deliverance. What are the fears, sins, or struggles that hold you captive? Trust that God's power to deliver is as real today as it was for the Israelites.

MOSES AND AMOS 3:7

The life of Moses exemplifies the truth of Amos 3:7: *"Surely the Sovereign Lord does nothing without revealing his plan to his servants the prophets."* Moses, one of the greatest prophets in Israel's history, was privy to God's plans and purposes, which were revealed to him directly.

God communicated with Moses in a unique and intimate manner, speaking to him *"face to face, as one speaks to a friend"* (Exodus 33:11). Before leading the Israelites out of Egypt, God revealed His plan for liberation to Moses through the burning bush, giving him specific instructions and promises (Exodus 3:1-10). Throughout the Exodus journey, God continued to disclose His intentions and guidance to Moses, including the giving of the Law on Mount Sinai and the plans for the Tabernacle.

Moses' life exemplifies the principle in Amos 3:7, demonstrating that God indeed reveals His plans to His prophets, ensuring that His will is communicated and enacted through their obedience and leadership. Moses' prophetic role was crucial in guiding Israel according to God's revealed purposes, highlighting the vital function of prophetic revelation in God's work among His people.

Be honest with yourself and God about areas where you need deliverance. Earnestly seek God's deliverance through prayer. Ask Him to break the chains that bind you. Use God's Word as a weapon against the enemy. Verses like John 8:36, *"So if the Son sets you free, you will be free indeed,"* can be powerful declarations of faith. Don't walk the journey alone. Find a community of believers who can support you in prayer and accountability. Recognize and celebrate the small steps of freedom you experience. This builds faith and perseverance.

Faith is crucial in experiencing God's deliverance. When Moses led the Israelites through the Red Sea, it was an act of faith. They had to trust God to divide the waters so they could cross on dry ground. *"By faith the people passed through the Red Sea as on dry land; but when the Egyptians tried to do so, they were drowned" (Hebrews 11:29).*

This faith in God's power and promise is what enabled them to experience such a miraculous deliverance. Take time to reflect on your own journey of faith. Are there areas where your faith needs strengthening? How can you cultivate a deeper trust in God's power to deliver you?

Our prayers for guidance and deliverance must align with Scripture. God's Word is a lamp to our feet and a light to our path (Psalm 119:105). It provides the foundation and direction for our prayers. *"Trust in the Lord with all your heart and lean not on your own understanding; in all your ways submit to him, and he will make your paths straight"* (Proverbs 3:5-6). *"I will instruct you and teach you in the way you should go; I will counsel you with my loving eye on you"* (Psalm 32:8). *"Whether you turn to the right or to the left, your ears will hear a voice behind you, saying, 'This is the way; walk in it'"* (Isaiah 30:21). *"So if the Son sets you free, you will be free indeed"* (John 8:36). *"Now the Lord is the Spirit, and where the Spirit of the Lord is, there is freedom"* (2 Corinthians 3:17).

Moses' life is a profound example of guidance and deliverance. His journey from Egypt to the Promised Land was marked by divine intervention, miraculous deliverance, and unwavering faith in God's promises. As we seek God's guidance and deliverance in our own lives, let us remember Moses' example and trust that the same God who led him will lead us.

Reflect on the lessons from Moses' life. Seek God's guidance in every decision, trust in His promises, and believe in His power to deliver you from all that holds you captive.

RED SEA MOMENT

I recall a Red Sea Moment in my life. I did not have to cross the Red Sea. But a Transition was happening. It was a change of jobs.

For fourteen years, I had worked in the Cardiac Rehabilitation department at a local hospital. Our family was young, and growing. During these years, my husband and I raised a wonderful young boy.

I dearly loved the job. And I was highly trained for this job. After a heart attack or a heart procedure, a patient would come to the rehabilitation program. For me, it was rewarding watching my clients recover from major surgery.

But things began to change at the hospital. There were rumors of many people being laid off in numerous departments. I had so hoped that it would not happen to us.

However, one day that **pink slip** came. I had a young child. We had just built a house. I had to work.

Before my open Bible, I asked the Holy Spirit to show me how to pray.

The instructions I received were as follows:

"For the next 30 days, sit quietly, with a heart to listen. Every day, sit for 40 minutes. There are to be no distractions, and no talking. Just wait, and listen!

A scripture that confirmed these instructions was given to me.

"Since ancient times no one has heard,
    no ear has perceived,
no eye has seen any God besides you,
    who acts on behalf of those who wait for him."
(Isaiah 64:4)

After thirty days of waiting, a wonderful job opportunity opened for me. It was very similar to the Rehabilitation job. And it was only thirty minutes from my house!

The staff were very kind and worked well together.

Waiting confidently on God, is a key to opening doors of opportunity!

REFLECTION QUESTIONS

1. Reflecting on Moses' initial hesitation and eventual trust in God's promises, what are some areas in your life where you feel hesitant or doubtful? How can you strengthen your trust in God's promises in those areas?

2. Consider the practical steps mentioned for seeking God's guidance. Which of these steps do you currently practice, and which could you incorporate more into your daily routine? How might these practices change your decision-making process?

3. Moses demonstrated unwavering faith when leading the Israelites through the Red Sea. Are there "Red Sea moments" in your life where you need to exercise greater faith in God's deliverance? How can you cultivate such faith?

4. How can you ensure that your prayers for guidance and deliverance align more closely with Scripture? Are there specific Bible verses that resonate with your current life situations and can guide your prayers?

5. Reflect on Moses' obedience despite his initial doubts. Are there areas in your life where you feel God is calling you to act, but you are

hesitant? What steps can you take to move forward in obedience, trusting in God's guidance and deliverance?

Prayer

Lord, we come to You in faith, believing that You are the same yesterday, today, and forever. Just as You guided and delivered Moses, we ask that You guide and deliver us. Lead us through our own wilderness, part the seas that stand in our way, and bring us into the freedom and promise that You have prepared for us. In Jesus' name, Amen.

3

AMOS - JUSTICE AND RIGHTEOUSNESS

Amos, a humble shepherd from Tekoa, emerges as a powerful voice for justice and righteousness in the Bible. His prophetic ministry, marked by bold declarations and unwavering commitment, addresses the rampant social injustices and moral decay of his time. Unlike many other prophets, Amos was not from a prophetic lineage nor was he initially a part of the religious establishment. This outsider status gave his messages an unfiltered and raw quality, directly confronting the complacency and corruption of Israel's elite. Amos's prophecies remind us that God deeply cares about how we treat one another, calling us to reflect His justice and righteousness in our daily lives.

The central themes of Amos's messages revolve around the need for social justice, genuine worship, and moral integrity. He passionately condemns the exploitation of the poor, the perversion of justice, and the hypocrisy of empty religious rituals. Through his vivid imagery and compelling rhetoric, Amos paints a stark picture of a society that has strayed far from God's standards. Yet, his call is not just a rebuke but also an invitation to repentance and transformation. As we delve into the life and messages of Amos, we are challenged to examine our own hearts and communities, seeking to align our actions with God's call for justice, mercy, and true righteousness.

THE CALL TO SOCIAL JUSTICE

Amos' time was marked by economic prosperity but moral and spiritual decay. The people of Israel enjoyed wealth and comfort, but it came at the expense of the poor and the oppressed. The rich exploited the vulnerable, and justice was perverted. Into this context, Amos brought a message that was as much a denunciation of injustice as it was a call to repentance.

"But let justice roll on like a river, righteousness like a never-failing stream!" (Amos 5:24). This verse encapsulates the heart of Amos' message. He was deeply concerned with the way society treated its most vulnerable members. He saw that true worship of God was inseparable from how we treat one another.

Amos' critique of Israel was not just about their religious rituals but about their everyday actions. He condemned those who "sell the innocent for silver, and the needy for a pair of sandals" (Amos 2:6). This was a society where the pursuit of wealth led to the dehumanization of the poor. Amos' words challenge us to reflect on our own societies and ask whether we, too, are guilty of valuing wealth over human dignity.

SPEAKING OUT AGAINST INJUSTICE

Amos' courage to speak out against injustice, despite being an outsider, is a profound lesson for us today. He was not part of the religious elite; he was a shepherd and a farmer. Yet, he did not shy away from delivering God's message of justice. His story reminds us that God can use anyone, regardless of their background, to bring about change.

"I was neither a prophet nor the son of a prophet, but I was a shepherd, and I also took care of sycamore-fig trees. But the Lord took me from tending the flock and said to me, 'Go, prophesy to my people Israel.'" (Amos 7:14-15). Amos' humble background did not prevent him from speaking truth to power. In fact, it may have given him a unique perspective on the injustices he witnessed.

Amos was uniquely positioned to observe and understand the struggles of the common people. His rural background allowed him to see firsthand the exploitation and oppression faced by the marginalized. This perspective fueled his passionate denunciations of the wealthy and powerful who trampled the needy and corrupted justice for personal gain. Amos' messages were not just about denouncing wrongdoing but calling for a transformation of heart and society, urging people to "let justice roll on like a river, righteousness like a never-failing stream" (Amos 5:24).

We, too, are called to speak out against injustice. This might mean challenging unfair practices in our workplaces, standing up for those who cannot defend themselves, or advocating for policies that protect the vulnerable. It requires humility and courage, recognizing that our strength comes from God, not our status. Speaking out against injustice is not just about raising our voices; it's about taking actionable steps to create a fairer and more just society. This could involve volunteering for organizations that support the disadvantaged, educating ourselves and others about systemic inequalities, or even just being a compassionate and listening ear to those who suffer from injustice.

Amos' example shows us that one does not need a prestigious position or title to make a difference. What is required is a heart attuned to God's justice and the courage to act on His behalf. Just as Amos was taken from his humble occupation to confront the injustices of his day, we must be willing to step out of our comfort zones to address the wrongs we see around us. This commitment to justice is a reflection of our faith and a testament to our trust in God's righteousness and love for all people.

PRAYING FOR JUSTICE

Prayer is a powerful tool in the fight for justice. Through prayer, we align our hearts with God's heart, and we seek His guidance and strength to act justly. Amos teaches us to pray for justice in our cities and communities, asking God to intervene where human systems fail.

"The Lord looked and was displeased that there was no justice. He saw that there was no one, he was appalled that there was no one to intervene; so his own arm achieved salvation for him, and his own righteousness sustained him" (Isaiah 59:15-16). This passage from Isaiah echoes the sentiment of Amos, highlighting God's deep concern for justice and His willingness to act when His people do not.

Praying for justice is not just about asking God to change external circumstances but also about seeking transformation within ourselves. When we pray for justice, we invite God to shape our hearts, giving us compassion for those who suffer and the courage to stand up for what is right. These prayers should be fervent and specific, addressing the various forms of injustice we witness—whether they are racial, economic, social, or environmental.

Our prayers should reflect a deep longing for God's justice to prevail. We must pray for the courage to act and the wisdom to know how best to intervene. We should also pray for those in positions of power, asking God to guide their decisions and inspire them to pursue righteousness. When we intercede for our leaders and lawmakers, we recognize that true justice is achieved when those who hold power are guided by divine wisdom and integrity.

Prayer can also be a source of comfort and strength for those who are oppressed. As we pray for justice, we should remember to lift up those who are suffering, asking God to provide them with resilience, hope, and support. By doing so, we stand in solidarity with the marginalized and oppressed, affirming their dignity and worth in the eyes of God.

Additionally, prayer can help us discern practical steps to take in the pursuit of justice. As we seek God's guidance, He may reveal specific actions we can take to address injustice in our own spheres of influence. This might include advocating for policy changes, volunteering with organizations that support the underserved, or educating ourselves and others about the issues at hand.

Incorporating prayer into our daily lives ensures that our efforts for justice are continually grounded in God's will. It reminds us that we are not alone in this struggle and that ultimate justice is in God's hands. As we persist in prayer, we draw closer to God, becoming more attuned to His desires for a just and righteous world.

WAYS TO ADVOCATE FOR JUSTICE

Advocating for justice requires both prayer and action. Here are some practical steps to help you engage in the pursuit of justice:

1. **Educate Yourself:** Learn about the issues of injustice in your community and around the world. Understanding the root causes of injustice can help you identify effective ways to address them.

2. **Support Fair Practices:** Choose to support businesses and organizations that promote fair trade and ethical practices. Your consumer choices can make a difference.

3. **Volunteer:** Get involved with local organizations that are working to combat injustice. Your time and skills can be valuable resources.

4. **Advocate:** Use your voice to advocate for policies that promote justice. Write to your elected officials and support initiatives that aim to create a more just society.

5. **Build Relationships:** Cultivate relationships with those who are different from you. Understanding and empathy are key to breaking down barriers and promoting justice.

ALIGNING PRAYERS WITH BIBLICAL JUSTICE

To ensure that our prayers and actions align with God's will, it is essential to ground them in Scripture. The Bible provides numerous examples and teachings on justice that can guide our prayers and actions.

One such example is the call of Isaiah. In Isaiah 6, we read about Isaiah's vision of the Lord and his commission to speak to the people. An angel touched Isaiah's lips with a live coal from the altar, symbolizing purification and preparation for his prophetic mission. When God asked, *"Whom shall I send? And who will go for us?"* Isaiah responded, *"Here am I. Send me!"* (Isaiah 6:8). This passage emphasizes the importance of being willing and prepared to respond to God's call for justice.

Another powerful scripture is Micah 6:8, which succinctly captures God's requirement for His people: *"He has shown you, O mortal, what is good. And what does the Lord require of you? To act justly and to love mercy and to walk humbly with your God."* This verse is a clear directive to pursue justice, mercy, and humility in all aspects of life.

The message of Amos is as relevant today as it was in ancient Israel. We live in a world where injustice still prevails, and the gap between the rich and the poor continues to widen. Amos calls us to examine our own lives and the structures of our society, to repent of our complicity in injustice, and to work actively towards a more just world.

Reflect on your own life and community. Are there areas where you see injustice? How can you, like Amos, speak out and act to address these issues? It might be through advocacy, supporting ethical businesses, volunteering, or simply by being more conscious of the ways your actions affect others.

Amos also reminds us that justice is not just a social issue but a deeply spiritual one. True justice flows from a heart aligned with God's values. It requires us to love our neighbors as ourselves and to see every person as made in the image of God. This perspective transforms our approach to justice, making it not just about fixing systems but about healing relationships and restoring dignity.

As we pursue justice, let us also seek God's guidance and strength. It is easy to become discouraged or overwhelmed by the magnitude of the problems we face. But remember that we do not act alone. God is with us, and He is deeply invested in the cause of justice. He will provide the wisdom, courage, and resources we need.

AMOS AND ISAIAH'S CALL

The calling of Isaiah, as described in Isaiah 6, offers a profound parallel to the ministry of Amos. In Isaiah's vision, an angel touched his lips with a live coal from the altar, purifying him and preparing him for his prophetic mission. This moment of cleansing was followed by God's pivotal question: *"Whom shall I send? And who will go for us?"* (Isaiah 6:8). Isaiah responded with willingness and humility: *"Here am I. Send me!"*

Amos, like Isaiah, received a divine calling to prophesy, though his background was markedly different. Amos was not a prophet by lineage or training; he was a shepherd and a fig tree farmer. Yet, God called him to deliver a critical message to Israel. Amos accepted this calling with the same readiness as Isaiah, demonstrating that God's call can come to anyone, regardless of their background or status.

Both Amos and Isaiah answered God's question, "Who will go for us?" with their lives and actions, showing that prophetic missions require a heart ready to respond to God's call. Their stories remind us that God seeks willing servants to carry His messages, and He equips those He calls, purifying and preparing them for their tasks, just as He did with Isaiah and Amos.

THE POWER OF HUMILITY

Amos' story also teaches us about the power of humility in the pursuit of justice. Despite being called to a significant prophetic role, Amos remained humble, always acknowledging his origins as a shepherd and farmer. This humility gave him a unique credibility and authenticity that resonated with the people.

Amos' humility is evident in his own words: *"I was neither a prophet nor the son of a prophet, but I was a shepherd, and I also took care of sycamore-fig trees. But the Lord took me from tending the flock and said to me, 'Go, prophesy to my people Israel'"* (Amos 7:14-15). By acknowledging his humble beginnings, Amos connected with the common people and demonstrated that God can use anyone, regardless of their background, to bring about significant change. This authenticity made his message more impactful and relatable to those he was called to address.

We are reminded that humility is crucial when addressing issues of justice. It keeps us grounded and open to learning from others, especially those who are directly affected by injustice. When we approach justice work with humility, we acknowledge that we don't have all the answers and that we need to listen to the voices of those who experience injustice firsthand. This posture of humility fosters genuine relationships and collaborative efforts, making our pursuit of justice more effective and inclusive.

Humility helps us to act not out of a desire for recognition but out of a genuine concern for others and a commitment to God's will. It shifts our focus from seeking personal accolades to serving others selflessly. This aligns our actions with the heart of Christ, who exemplified ultimate humility and servanthood. True justice work is not about elevating ourselves but about lifting up those who are oppressed and marginalized.

Humility also involves recognizing our own limitations and the need for God's help. We are not the saviors of the world; God is. Our role is to be faithful and obedient to His call, trusting that He will bring about the ultimate justice. Humility reminds us that we are part of a larger divine plan, and while our efforts are important, they are just a piece of God's overarching work in the world. This understanding can alleviate the pressure we might feel to solve every problem ourselves and help us rely more on God's guidance and power.

Humility also fosters a spirit of repentance and reflection. It encourages us to examine our own biases and complicity in systems of injustice. By acknowledging our imperfections and seeking God's forgiveness, we become more effective agents of change. Humility helps us to see the broader picture and recognize that everyone, including ourselves, is in need of God's grace and redemption.

Amos' story displays the power of humility in pursuing justice. By remaining humble, we stay connected to those we serve, act out of genuine compassion, recognize our need for God's help, and continuously seek personal growth and understanding. Humility allows us to work for justice not with an attitude of superiority, but with a heart aligned with God's love and a commitment to His will.

A PRAYER FOR JUSTICE

As we close this chapter, let us commit to being advocates for justice, following the example of Amos. Let us pray for God's guidance, strength, and wisdom as we seek to address the injustices in our world.

Heavenly Father, we thank You for the example of Amos, who spoke out boldly for justice and righteousness. We ask for Your guidance as we seek to address the injustices in our own lives and communities. Give us the courage to speak truth to power, the wisdom to know how best to act, and the humility to recognize our dependence on You. Let justice roll on like a river and righteousness like a never-failing stream in our world today. In Jesus' name, Amen.

As we continue our journey through the lives of the prophets, let the story of Amos inspire us to live out our faith through acts of justice and compassion. Let us be the hands and feet of God in a world that desperately needs His justice and love.

THE 10,000 THIEF

College was exciting for me. I loved to learn. To listen to powerful lectures and to study new material was a passion for me. I especially enjoyed the field of Physiology.

I obtained my Undergraduate Degree, and a Master's Degree, yet I longed for another degree that would allow me to work in a more flexible manner,

For over a year, I pursued this degree. To do so, I had to work part-time, and study at night. Soon, I would finish, for only 3 semesters were left. Of course, I did not qualify for any aid, and had to borrow $10,000.

All was well until one instructor targeted me. Finally, she succeeded in terminating my studies. After, I received this devasting news, I walked to my car with a broken heart.

How would my family pay off this debt? Could I possibly appeal? Was there any action to take?

I did obtain a lawyer. After, the lawyer reviewed my case, she suggested that I just drop it. The fight for my money would cost more than the debt!

I am sure that other people have been left without college degrees.

I knew that the only answer for me, would be found in prayer.

As I prayed about it, the Holy Spirit revealed a few scriptures to me.

"If I would forgive, the Lord would take care of me. If I did not forgive, I would block blessings from heaven."

From the Lord's Prayer:

"And forgive us our debts,
as we also have forgiven our debtors."
(Matthew 6:12)

A few years passed, and our family experienced some great financial miracles.

One year, my husband was given a $10,000 bonus. Truly that was a miracle for us.

And of even greater significance, when the COVID -19 epidemic occurred, I would have been working directly in a HIGH- RISK environment. GOD protected me from a future danger!

REFLECTION QUESTIONS

1. **Personal Responsibility in Justice:** Reflecting on Amos' call to address societal injustices, what specific injustices do you observe in your community or society? How can you take personal responsibility to advocate for change in these areas?

2. **Courage to Speak Out:** Amos, despite his humble background, boldly spoke out against the injustices of his time. Are there situations in your life where you feel called to speak out but are hesitant? What steps can you take to find the courage to speak truth to power?

3. **Aligning Actions with Faith:** Amos emphasized that true worship of God is inseparable from how we treat others. In what ways can you ensure that your daily actions and decisions reflect your faith and commitment to justice and righteousness?

4. **Praying for Justice:** How can you incorporate prayers for justice into your regular prayer life? What specific injustices will you commit to praying about, and how can you ask for God's guidance and intervention in these areas?

5. **Humility in Advocacy:** Amos demonstrated humility in his prophetic role. How can you practice humility in your efforts to promote justice? What steps can you take to ensure that your actions are motivated by genuine concern for others rather than a desire for recognition or personal gain?

4

ISAIAH - VISION AND HOPE

Isaiah, often referred to as the "Prince of Prophets," stands out as one of the most influential voices in the Bible. His prophetic ministry spanned the reigns of four kings of Judah, and his messages were filled with powerful visions of judgment and redemption. Isaiah's prophecies offer profound insights into the themes of vision and hope, as he vividly portrayed the coming of the Messiah and the ultimate restoration of God's people. Through his writings, we are invited to see beyond our present circumstances and trust in the promises of a faithful God who brings light out of darkness and hope out of despair.

Isaiah's life and prophecies challenge us to maintain hope in God's promises, even when faced with overwhelming challenges. His vision of a suffering servant, who would bear the sins of many, pointed to Jesus Christ and offered a glimpse of God's redemptive plan for humanity. Isaiah's messages are not only relevant for his time but also resonate deeply with our own lives today, calling us to trust in God's unchanging promises and to find strength and encouragement in His word. As we delve into Isaiah's story, we are reminded that God's vision for our lives is filled with hope and His plans for us are always for our good.

ISAIAH'S CALLING AND PROPHETIC VISION

Isaiah's prophetic journey began with a profound vision of the Lord. In the year that King Uzziah died, Isaiah saw the Lord sitting on a throne, high and exalted, with the train of His robe filling the temple. Seraphim were in attendance, calling out, *"Holy, holy, holy is the Lord Almighty; the whole earth is full of His glory"* (Isaiah 6:3). This vision of God's majesty and holiness left Isaiah acutely aware of his own unworthiness.

"Woe to me!" I cried. "I am ruined! For I am a man of unclean lips, and I live among a people of unclean lips, and my eyes have seen the King, the Lord Almighty" (Isaiah 6:5). Yet, in this moment of despair, one of the seraphim flew to Isaiah with a live coal from the altar, touching his lips and declaring that his guilt was taken away and his sin atoned for.

This transformative encounter not only cleansed Isaiah but also commissioned him for his prophetic mission. When the Lord asked, *"Whom shall I send? And who will go for us?"* Isaiah responded, *"Here am I. Send me!"*

(Isaiah 6:8). Isaiah's readiness to respond to God's call, despite his initial fear, exemplifies the heart of a true servant of God.

PROPHECIES OF HOPE AND REDEMPTION

Isaiah's prophecies were not limited to warnings and judgments. He also delivered some of the most profound messages of hope and redemption in the entire Bible. His vision extended beyond the immediate circumstances of Israel and Judah to encompass the future coming of the Messiah and the ultimate restoration of God's people.

One of the most remarkable prophecies of hope is found in Isaiah 9: *"For to us a child is born, to us a son is given, and the government will be on his shoulders. And he will be called Wonderful Counselor, Mighty God, Everlasting Father, Prince of Peace"* (Isaiah 9:6). This prophecy foretold the birth of Jesus Christ, offering a vision of a future where peace and justice would prevail.

Isaiah also spoke of a time when God would create new heavens and a new earth. *"See, I will create new heavens and a new earth. The former things will not be remembered, nor will they come to mind. But be glad and rejoice forever in what I will create"* (Isaiah 65:17-18). This promise of ultimate renewal and restoration provides a powerful source of hope for believers facing trials and uncertainties.

MAINTAINING HOPE IN DIFFICULT TIMES

Isaiah's prophecies were delivered during times of great political and social upheaval. The northern kingdom of Israel had fallen to Assyria, and Judah faced constant threats from powerful empires. In such turbulent times, maintaining hope can be challenging. Yet, Isaiah's unwavering faith in God's promises serves as a beacon of hope for us today.

In our own lives, we encounter seasons of difficulty and uncertainty. It is during these times that we must hold fast to the promises of God, just as Isaiah did. Isaiah's words remind us that God is sovereign, and His plans for us are filled with hope and a future. *"For I know the plans I have for you," declares the Lord, "plans to prosper you and not to harm you, plans to give you hope and a future"* (Jeremiah 29:11).

To maintain hope in difficult times, we must immerse ourselves in God's Word, seek His presence in prayer, and surround ourselves with a community of faith. Scripture is replete with promises of God's faithfulness and love, which can sustain us through the darkest times.

PRAYING FOR VISION AND HOPE

Isaiah's life and ministry teach us the importance of seeking God's vision and holding on to hope. Prophetic prayer is a powerful way to align our hearts with God's purposes and to seek His guidance and comfort. When we pray for vision and hope, we invite God to reveal His plans for our lives and to fill us with the assurance of His promises.

One of the most inspiring prayers for vision and hope is found in Isaiah 40: *"But those who hope in the Lord will renew their strength. They will soar on wings like eagles; they will run and not grow weary, they will walk and not be faint"* (Isaiah 40:31). This verse encourages us to place our hope in the Lord, knowing that He will renew our strength and enable us to persevere.

When praying for vision, ask God to open your eyes to see His purposes and plans. Seek His guidance for the path ahead and trust that He will lead you. For hope, ask God to fill your heart with His promises and to strengthen your faith. Trust that He is working all things together for your good, even when the outcome is not yet visible.

PRACTICAL STEPS FOR CULTIVATING VISION AND HOPE

To cultivate vision and hope in our lives, we must be intentional in our spiritual practices. Here are some practical steps to help you grow in these areas:

1. **Daily Devotion:** Spend time each day in prayer and Bible reading. Let God's Word shape your perspective and fill you with His promises.

2. **Journaling:** Write down your prayers, reflections, and any insights you receive from God. This practice can help you track your spiritual growth and recognize God's work in your life.

3. **Community:** Engage with a faith community that encourages and supports you. Share your struggles and victories with others, and draw strength from their experiences.

4. **Service:** Serve others in your community. Helping those in need can shift your focus from your own challenges to the broader work of God's kingdom.

5. **Rest:** Take time to rest and recharge. Physical rest is essential for spiritual well-being, allowing you to hear God's voice more clearly.

THE ROLE OF PROPHECY IN PROVIDING VISION

Isaiah's prophecies were not just about foretelling future events; they were about providing a vision that would sustain God's people through difficult times. Prophetic vision lifts our eyes from our present circumstances to the greater reality of God's kingdom. It reminds us that our story is part of God's larger narrative of redemption.

Isaiah's vision of the suffering servant in Isaiah 53 is a profound example of this. He foretold the coming of Jesus, who would take on the sins of the world and bring healing and salvation. *"But he was pierced for our transgressions, he was crushed for our iniquities; the punishment that brought us peace was on him, and by his wounds we are healed"* (Isaiah 53:5). This prophecy provided hope to those who longed for redemption and remains a cornerstone of Christian faith.

Prophetic vision can also provide guidance for our personal lives. When we seek God's vision, we ask Him to reveal His plans and purposes for us. This can come through prayer, scripture, and the counsel of wise and godly mentors. It requires us to be open and attentive to the Holy Spirit's leading.

ISAIAH AND EZEKIEL 37

In Ezekiel 37, the prophet Ezekiel is commanded to speak life to dry bones and to prophesy to the wind, symbolizing God's power to restore and revive His people. This vivid imagery of transformation and renewal resonates deeply with the ministry of Isaiah.

Isaiah's prophecies also spoke of renewal and hope, particularly in times of despair. He foretold the coming of the Messiah, a shoot from the stump of Jesse, bringing justice, peace, and restoration (Isaiah 11:1-10). Isaiah's messages often conveyed God's promise to breathe new life into His people, transforming their desolation into a vibrant future.

Both prophets illustrate the profound power of God's word to bring life and hope. Isaiah's prophecies, like Ezekiel's vision, remind us that no situation is beyond God's ability to redeem and restore. Through His prophets, God speaks life into our circumstances, calling us to trust in His power to bring renewal and transformation.

LIVING WITH ETERNAL HOPE

Isaiah's prophecies also point us toward the ultimate hope of eternal life with God. His vision of new heavens and a new earth offers a glimpse of the future that awaits us. *"See, I will create new heavens and a new earth. The former things will not be remembered, nor will they come to mind"* (Isaiah 65:17). This eternal perspective helps us to endure present trials with the assurance that God's promises are sure and His plans for us are good. Isaiah's vivid imagery of a restored creation where peace, justice, and righteousness reign is a powerful reminder that our current struggles are temporary, and God's ultimate plan is one of renewal and everlasting joy.

Living with eternal hope means keeping our focus on the things that matter most. It means prioritizing our relationship with God, loving others, and living out the values of God's kingdom. This eternal perspective transforms our daily lives, guiding our decisions, actions, and interactions with others. It encourages us to invest in what is eternal rather than what is fleeting. This mindset shapes our character, making us more patient, compassionate, and steadfast in our faith. Knowing that our ultimate home is with God, we can face life's challenges with a sense of peace and purpose, trusting that every moment is part of God's greater plan.

It also means trusting that God is at work, even when we cannot see the full picture. Isaiah's prophecies often spoke of future events that would take generations to fulfill, reminding us that God's timing is perfect. *"For my thoughts are not your thoughts, neither are your ways my ways," declares the Lord. "As the heavens are higher than the earth, so are my ways higher than your ways and my thoughts than your thoughts"* (Isaiah 55:8-9). This trust in God's overarching plan allows us to live with hope and confidence, even in the midst of uncertainty. We can rest in the knowledge that God is sovereign, and His purposes will ultimately prevail.

As we live with this eternal hope, we are called to share it with others. Isaiah's message was not just for his own time; it was for all generations. We, too, are called to be messengers of hope, proclaiming the good news of God's love and redemption to a world in need. This involves more than just words; it requires us to live in a way that reflects the hope we profess. By embodying the values of God's kingdom—justice, mercy, humility, and love—we become living testimonies of the hope that is within us. Our lives should invite others to seek the same eternal hope that anchors us.

Sharing eternal hope means being a light in the darkness, offering encouragement to those who are weary, and pointing them to the promises of God. It means showing compassion to those who are hurting and offering them the comfort of God's presence. In a world often marked by despair and uncertainty, our unwavering hope can be a powerful testimony to the faithfulness of God. Isaiah's vision of a future filled with God's glory inspires us to actively participate in God's redemptive work here and now, bringing glimpses of His kingdom to earth as we await its full realization.

Living with eternal hope transforms not only our perspective but also our impact on the world around us. As we focus on God's promises and align our lives with His eternal purposes, we become beacons of hope, reflecting His love and grace to others. Let Isaiah's vision of a new heavens and a new earth encourage you to live with an eternal perspective, trusting in God's promises and sharing His hope with those around you.

A PRAYER FOR VISION AND HOPE

Let us conclude this chapter with a prayer, asking God to fill us with His vision and hope. May we be inspired by Isaiah's example and strengthened by God's promises.

Heavenly Father, we thank You for the life and ministry of Isaiah, who proclaimed Your vision and hope to a weary world. We ask that You open our eyes to see Your purposes and plans for our lives. Fill us with hope, even in the midst of difficulties, and remind us of Your faithful promises. Strengthen our faith and renew our strength, so that we may run and not grow weary, walk and not be faint. Help us to live with an eternal perspective, trusting in Your goodness and sharing Your hope with others. In Jesus' name, Amen.

As we continue our journey through the lives of the prophets, let the story of Isaiah inspire us to seek God's vision and hold on to hope. May we be encouraged to live out our faith with the assurance that God's promises are true and His plans for us are filled with hope and a future.

THE TOUCH OF AN ANGEL

During a two -year period that I helped lead Community Prayer Meetings, several heavenly encounters occurred to me. God's Presence was so powerful during these prayer meetings.

It all began when I participated with a zealous group of Intercessors at Bluefield, WV.

At least two nights a month, we prayed ALL NIGHT. We kept the NIGHT WATCH for our community. Those all- night meetings were awesome. The time went by so quickly. It was dawn before we knew it!

I helped lead a Prayer Thrust with several churches in our region. About twice a month, at least 5 to 12 churches sent pastors and intercessors to these meetings. We prayed for the community, for the businesses, and for the leaders.

Spiritual warfare was also present. Several times, I faced some great threats, but no harm occurred. Also, attempts were made to stop these prayer meetings, but they were not halted.

One night, I came home and lay on the couch. I was exhausted. I needed to fix a meal, but was too tired to get up. I feel into a deep sleep and was awakened by a TOUCH.

It was not just any type of touch. A very large angel, was touching my right shoulder. He was a war-angel. He was dressed as a warrior. I could tell that he had a very large sword, and he was protected by a brass-type of clothing.

Strength began to surge in my body. My senses were alerted. And I looked at this angel. But he would only be seen for a brief period.

This experience ignited greater passion to pursue personal prayer and intercession for others, including the communities and the nation.

"Praise the Lord, you his angels,
*   you mighty ones who do his bidding,*
*   who obey his word."*
(Psalm 103:20)

REFLECTION QUESTIONS

1. Reflecting on Isaiah's immediate response to God's call, *"Here am I. Send me!"* (Isaiah 6:8), how do you respond when you feel God calling you to a specific task or mission? What steps can you take to be more open and responsive to His call in your life?

2. Isaiah delivered messages of hope during turbulent times. In your own life, how do you maintain hope when facing difficult circumstances? What scriptures or practices help you stay anchored in God's promises?

3. Isaiah's prophecies provided a vision for the future. Have you sought God's vision for your life? How can you cultivate a clearer sense of His direction and purpose for you through prayer and reflection?

4. Isaiah's message was not only for his time but for future generations. How can you be a messenger of hope to those around you? In what ways can you share the good news of God's love and redemption with others in your community?

5. Isaiah's vision of new heavens and a new earth offers an eternal perspective. How does this eternal hope influence your daily decisions and priorities? What changes can you make to live more intentionally with an eternal perspective in mind?

5

JEREMIAH - PERSEVERANCE AND RESTORATION

Jeremiah, often known as the "Weeping Prophet," offers a profound and powerful perspective on faithfulness and perseverance. His ministry, which spanned over four decades during one of the most turbulent periods in Judah's history, was marked by relentless opposition, persecution, and personal sacrifice. Despite the overwhelming challenges, Jeremiah remained steadfast in his commitment to proclaim God's truth, demonstrating an unwavering dedication to his prophetic calling. His life and messages provide powerful lessons on the importance of enduring faith, trusting in God's promises, and seeking His restoration in the midst of trials.

Jeremiah's prophecies are filled with themes of judgment and hope, reflecting God's deep sorrow over His people's unfaithfulness and His unwavering desire to restore them. Through Jeremiah's lamentations and heartfelt prayers, we gain insight into the struggle of the remaining faithful when faced with adversity. Yet, amid the warnings of impending exile, Jeremiah also brought messages of hope and a promise of a new covenant—a future where God's laws would be written on the hearts of His people. As we explore the life and ministry of Jeremiah, we are encouraged to persevere in our faith, trusting that God is with us through every challenge and that His plans for us are rooted in His everlasting love.

JEREMIAH'S CALL AND MINISTRY

Jeremiah's prophetic ministry began with a powerful encounter with God. Called from a young age, Jeremiah was chosen to deliver God's messages to a rebellious and unrepentant nation. God's words to Jeremiah were both daunting and reassuring: *"Before I formed you in the womb I knew you, before you were born I set you apart; I appointed you as a prophet to the nations"* (Jeremiah 1:5). Despite his initial reluctance and feelings of inadequacy, Jeremiah accepted God's call, trusting in His divine purpose.

"Do not say, 'I am too young.' You must go to everyone I send you to and say whatever I command you. Do not be afraid of them, for I am with you and will rescue you," declares the Lord (Jeremiah 1:7-8). With these words, God assured Jeremiah of His presence and protection,

setting the stage for a prophetic ministry that would span over four decades.

Jeremiah's ministry was one of relentless perseverance. He faced constant opposition, rejection, and persecution from the very people he was sent to warn. His messages of impending judgment and calls for repentance were met with hostility and disbelief. Yet, despite the overwhelming adversity, Jeremiah remained steadfast, driven by a deep conviction in God's truth and a compassionate heart for his people.

THE POWER OF PERSEVERANCE

Jeremiah's life is a testament to the power of perseverance. He endured physical threats, imprisonment, and social ostracism. His perseverance was not rooted in human strength but in his unwavering faith in God's promises. Jeremiah's ability to persevere through such trials encourages us to remain faithful and resilient in the face of our own challenges.

"But the Lord is with me like a mighty warrior; so my persecutors will stumble and not prevail. They will fail and be thoroughly disgraced; their dishonor will never be forgotten" (Jeremiah 20:11). This verse encapsulates Jeremiah's confidence in God's protection and justice, even when his circumstances seemed insurmountable.

Perseverance is essential in our spiritual journey. It is easy to become discouraged when we face trials, but Jeremiah's example reminds us that God is with us, strengthening us and guiding us through every difficulty. Our perseverance is a testament to our faith and trust in God's promises.

A MESSAGE OF HOPE AND RESTORATION

While Jeremiah's prophecies often focused on judgment, they also contained powerful messages of hope and restoration. Despite the imminent destruction of Jerusalem and the exile of the Israelites, God promised to restore His people and renew their covenant relationship with Him.

One of the most beautiful promises of restoration is found in Jeremiah 29:11-14: *"For I know the plans I have for you," declares the Lord, "plans to prosper you and not to harm you, plans to give you hope and a future. Then you will call on me and come and pray to me, and I will listen to you. You will seek me and find me when you seek me with all your heart. I will be found by you," declares the Lord, "and will bring you back from captivity."* This promise assured the exiled Israelites that their suffering was not the end of their story. God had a plan for their future, a plan filled with hope and restoration.

Jeremiah also prophesied about the new covenant, a promise of a renewed relationship between God and His people: *"The days are coming," declares the Lord, "when I will make a new covenant with the people of Israel and with the people of Judah. It will not be like the covenant I made with their ancestors... I will put my law in their minds and write it on their hearts. I will be their God, and they will be my people"* (Jeremiah 31:31-33). This prophecy points to the ultimate restoration through Jesus Christ, who established the new covenant through His death and resurrection.

TRUSTING IN GOD'S PROMISES

Jeremiah's messages of hope and restoration are deeply relevant for us today. They remind us that no matter how bleak our circumstances may seem, God has a plan for our future. His plans are to prosper us and give us hope. Trusting in God's promises requires us to look beyond our immediate challenges and hold on to the assurance that God is at work, even when we cannot see it.

"Blessed is the one who trusts in the Lord, whose confidence is in him. They will be like a tree planted by the water that sends out its roots by the stream. It does not fear when heat comes; its leaves are always green. It has no worries in a year of drought and never fails to bear fruit" (Jeremiah 17:7-8). This imagery of a tree planted by the water illustrates the steadfastness and fruitfulness that come

from trusting in God. When we place our trust in Him, we are rooted and sustained by His unchanging love and faithfulness.

Jeremiah's prophecies often came during times of great turmoil and uncertainty. The people of Judah faced exile, destruction, and profound loss. Yet, amidst these dire predictions, Jeremiah consistently conveyed God's promise of eventual restoration and renewal. *"For I know the plans I have for you," declares the Lord, "plans to prosper you and not to harm you, plans to give you hope and a future"* (Jeremiah 29:11). This assurance was meant to anchor the people's faith in God's ultimate sovereignty and goodness, reminding them that their current suffering was not the end of the story.

Trusting in God's promises involves an active decision to focus on His faithfulness rather than our fears. It means choosing to believe in God's goodness even when circumstances seem to contradict it. Jeremiah's own life, filled with hardships and rejection, is a testament to this kind of trust. Despite his personal suffering, he continued to proclaim God's message, confident in the eventual fulfillment of God's promises. This kind of trust transforms our perspective, enabling us to see beyond our immediate struggles to the broader narrative of God's redemptive plan.

This trust is not passive; it requires us to actively root ourselves in God's word and presence. Just as a tree planted by the water sends out its roots to find sustenance, we too must seek nourishment from God's promises. Daily prayer, meditation on Scripture, and fellowship with other believers help reinforce our faith and remind us of God's unfailing love. These practices help us develop a resilient faith that can withstand the trials and uncertainties of life.

Trusting in God's promises empowers us to live with hope and purpose. When we are confident that God has good plans for us, we can approach life's challenges with a sense of peace and assurance. This trust enables us to take risks, step out in faith, and pursue the paths God has laid out for us, knowing that He is with us every step of the way. It also allows us to be a source of encouragement and hope to others, sharing with them the comfort and strength we have found in God's promises.

Jeremiah's message reminds us that God's timing and ways are often beyond our understanding, yet they are always for our good. *"But blessed is the one who trusts in the Lord, whose confidence is in him"* (Jeremiah 17:7). This confidence is not based on our circumstances but on the character of God Himself. Trusting in God's promises requires us to surrender our anxieties and uncertainties to Him, resting in the knowledge that He is faithful and His plans are perfect.

Trusting in God's promises means relying on His faithfulness and sovereignty, even in the face of adversity. It calls us to root ourselves deeply in His word, maintain hope amidst trials, and live with the assurance that God's plans for us are good. As we trust in Him, we become like trees planted by the water, steadfast and fruitful, drawing life and strength from His eternal promises.

PRAYING FOR PERSEVERANCE AND RESTORATION

Jeremiah's life teaches us the importance of prayer in times of perseverance and restoration. Through prayer, we can seek God's strength to endure trials and His guidance to navigate difficult circumstances. Prayer is also a powerful way to align our hearts with God's promises and to seek His restoration in our lives.

When we pray for perseverance, we acknowledge our dependence on God and ask for His strength to remain faithful. We can be honest about our struggles and ask God to renew our spirits and give us the resilience to continue. Praying for restoration involves seeking God's healing and renewal in areas of our lives that are broken or in need of repair. It is a declaration of our trust in His ability to restore and make all things new.

PRACTICAL STEPS FOR PERSEVERANCE AND RESTORATION

To cultivate perseverance and experience restoration in our lives, we can take practical steps that align us with God's purposes:

1. **Daily Surrender:** Start each day by surrendering your struggles and challenges to God. Ask for His strength and guidance to persevere through whatever comes your way.

2. **Scripture Meditation:** Immerse yourself in God's Word, focusing on passages that speak of His faithfulness and promises. Let His truth anchor your heart and mind.

3. **Prayer and Fasting:** Engage in regular prayer and fasting as a way to seek God's presence and power. Fasting can help you focus on God and depend on Him more deeply.

4. **Community Support:** Surround yourself with a community of believers who can support you in prayer and encouragement. Share your burdens and victories with others who can walk alongside you.

5. **Rest and Renewal:** Take time to rest and recharge. Physical and spiritual rest are essential

for maintaining perseverance. Allow God to refresh your spirit and renew your strength.

THE ROLE OF COMMUNITY IN PERSEVERANCE

Jeremiah's journey was marked by loneliness and isolation, yet he continued to persevere because of his unwavering faith in God's call. In contrast, we are encouraged to lean on the support of our faith community. The Apostle Paul reminds us of the importance of community in our spiritual journey: *"Carry each other's burdens, and in this way you will fulfill the law of Christ"* (Galatians 6:2). When we support one another, we strengthen our collective ability to persevere.

Building a supportive community involves being vulnerable and open about our struggles. It means asking for help when needed and offering support to others in their times of need. A strong community can provide the encouragement and accountability necessary to keep us grounded in our faith and committed to God's purposes.

EMBRACING GOD'S RESTORATION

Just as God promised restoration to the Israelites, He offers us restoration in every aspect of our lives. Whether we are dealing with broken relationships, health issues, financial struggles, or spiritual dryness, God's promise of restoration is available to us. Embracing this restoration involves trusting in God's timing and being open to the ways He chooses to bring healing and renewal.

One of the most powerful examples of restoration is the story of the prodigal son in Luke 15. The son, who had squandered his inheritance, returned to his father with a repentant heart, hoping to be received as a servant. Instead, the father ran to him, embraced him, and restored him as a beloved son. This parable illustrates God's immense love and His desire to restore us to a place of honor and relationship with Him.

"Therefore, if anyone is in Christ, the new creation has come: The old has gone, the new is here!" (2 Corinthians 5:17). This verse reassures us that through Christ, we are made new. Our past mistakes and failures do not define us; instead, we are defined by our identity in Christ and His redemptive work in our lives.

THE HOPE OF FUTURE RESTORATION

Jeremiah's prophecies of restoration also point us toward the ultimate restoration that will come with the return of Jesus Christ. In Revelation 21:4, we are given a vision of this future: *"He will wipe every tear from their eyes. There will be no more death or mourning or crying or pain, for the old order of things has passed away."* This promise of a restored creation gives us hope and encouragement to persevere through our present challenges.

Living with the hope of future restoration means keeping our eyes fixed on the eternal promises of God. It means trusting that He is working all things together for our good and that our present sufferings are not worth comparing with the glory that will be revealed in us (Romans 8:18).

A PRAYER FOR PERSEVERANCE AND RESTORATION

Let us close this chapter with a prayer, seeking God's strength to persevere and His grace to restore us in every area of our lives.

Heavenly Father, we thank You for the life and example of Jeremiah, who persevered through immense challenges and proclaimed Your promises of restoration. We ask for Your strength to persevere in our own trials and difficulties. Renew our spirits and give us the resilience to remain faithful. We trust in Your promises and ask for Your restoration in every area of our lives. Heal our brokenness, renew our hope, and restore our joy. Help us to live with an eternal perspective, keeping our eyes fixed on the hope of Your ultimate restoration. In Jesus' name, Amen.

As we continue our journey through the lives of the prophets, let the story of Jeremiah inspire us to persevere with faith and to embrace the restoration that God promises. May we be encouraged to trust in God's unchanging love and faithfulness, knowing that He is always at work in our lives, bringing about His good purposes.

THE VISION OF WATER FROM A ROCK

Waterfalls are majestic. On hiking trips, I have witnessed several gorgeous waterfalls.

Jesus speaks of The Living Water. His message refers to The Holy Spirit.

"On the last and greatest day of the festival, Jesus stood and said in a loud voice, 'Let anyone who is thirsty come to me and drink.
Whoever believes in me, as Scripture has said, rivers of living water will flow from within them.'"
(John 7:37-38)

During the two- year period of Night-Watch prayer meetings, I saw a scene of water flowing from a rock.

One Sunday morning, during a time of worship, The Holy Spirit could be sensed in the church service. My hands were raised, as I praised The Lord. Suddenly, an atmosphere of PEACE flooded my soul. It was like waves of an ocean, splashing upon me.

Then I saw it---a huge Spiritual Rock. It must have been a heavenly rock. This rock was sitting by the altar, close to the pulpit. From each side of the rock, heavenly water burst forth. Water flowed from two sides of the rock. Two streams of water flowed from the sides of the church. The streams flowed out of the door, into the parking lot.

For at least fifteen minutes, the heavenly waters flowed. My eyes were glued to that Heavenly Rock. It was so amazing. I was reminded of a scripture.

"He opened the rock, and water gushed out;
* it flowed like a river in the desert."* (Psalm 105:41)

REFLECTION QUESTIONS

1. Reflecting on Jeremiah's initial reluctance and eventual acceptance of God's call, are there areas in your life where you feel called by God but are hesitant to respond? What steps can you take to embrace God's call with trust and confidence?

2. Jeremiah's perseverance through immense challenges is inspiring. What personal trials are you currently facing that require perseverance? How can you draw strength from Jeremiah's example to remain steadfast in your faith?

3. Jeremiah's prophecies included powerful promises of restoration. Are there areas in your life that feel broken or in need of renewal? How can you trust God's promise of restoration and actively seek His healing and renewal?

4. Jeremiah often felt isolated in his ministry. How can you cultivate a supportive community around you that encourages perseverance and faithfulness? In what ways can you be a source of support for others in your community?

5. Reflect on the hope of future restoration that Jeremiah pointed to. How does living with an eternal perspective influence your daily decisions and outlook on life? What practices can you incorporate to keep your focus on God's promises and the hope of His ultimate restoration?

6

EZEKIEL - RENEWAL AND REBIRTH

Ezekiel, a prophet during the Babylonian exile, presents a vivid and compelling vision of renewal and rebirth. His prophetic ministry, marked by extraordinary visions and symbolic actions, was delivered to a people in despair, far from their homeland and feeling abandoned by God. Through Ezekiel, God communicated His plans for restoration, offering hope and a promise of new life to the exiled Israelites. Ezekiel's visions, such as the valley of dry bones coming to life, powerfully illustrate God's ability to bring renewal to the most desolate situations.

Ezekiel's messages are rich with symbolism and profound spiritual truths, calling us to embrace the transformative power of God's Spirit. His visions challenge us to believe in God's promise of renewal, even when our circumstances seem beyond hope. The prophet's life and ministry remind us that no situation is too dire for God to redeem, and that His plans for us

involve a complete restoration of heart and spirit. As we delve into the story of Ezekiel, we are invited to open our hearts to God's renewing power, trusting that He can bring life and hope to our most challenging circumstances.

EZEKIEL'S CALLING AND VISION

Ezekiel was a priest who was taken into Babylonian captivity along with many other Israelites. It was during this exile that God called him to be a prophet. Ezekiel's prophetic journey began with an extraordinary vision by the Kebar River. He saw a stormy wind, a great cloud with flashing fire, and four living creatures with the likeness of a man, each with four faces and four wings. Above them was a throne, and seated on the throne was a figure like that of a man. *"This was the appearance of the likeness of the glory of the Lord. When I saw it, I fell facedown, and I heard the voice of one speaking"* (Ezekiel 1:28).

This vision of God's glory was overwhelming and set the stage for Ezekiel's prophetic ministry. The sheer magnificence and power of the vision conveyed the holiness and sovereignty of God, emphasizing that Ezekiel's message came directly from the divine throne. The vision also signaled the weight and seriousness of his calling, highlighting that Ezekiel was to be a messenger of profound and often challenging truths. In this encounter, God's glory was not confined to the temple in Jerusalem but was present even in exile, reassuring the Israelites of His omnipresence and ongoing involvement in their lives.

God spoke to Ezekiel, commissioning him to speak to the rebellious house of Israel. *"Son of man, I am sending you to the Israelites, to a rebellious nation that has rebelled against me; they and their ancestors have been in revolt against me to this very day"* (Ezekiel 2:3). Despite the daunting task, Ezekiel was empowered by God's Spirit to deliver His messages. This divine commissioning revealed the difficult nature of Ezekiel's mission. He was to confront a nation that had consistently turned away from God, delivering messages of judgment and calls for repentance.

The imagery in Ezekiel's vision is rich with symbolism. The four living creatures with their multiple faces and wings represent the comprehensive nature of God's vision and authority, spanning all directions and encompassing all aspects of creation. The wheels within wheels and the eyes covering them illustrate God's omnipresence and omniscience, signifying that nothing escapes His notice. This powerful imagery served to reassure Ezekiel of God's absolute sovereignty and provided the foundation for the prophet's unwavering confidence in his mission.

Ezekiel's initial reaction to the vision—falling face-down—demonstrates his deep reverence and recognition of God's overwhelming majesty. This humility and awe would characterize Ezekiel's ministry, as he continually sought to convey the gravity of God's messages to a stubborn and often unresponsive audience. Despite the resistance he faced, Ezekiel's commitment to his prophetic role never wavered, bolstered by the profound experience of God's presence and glory.

The calling of Ezekiel also involved a symbolic act where he was instructed to eat a scroll containing God's words. *"Then he said to me, 'Son of man, eat what is before you, eat this scroll; then go and speak to the people of Israel.' So I opened my mouth, and he gave me the scroll to eat"* (Ezekiel 3:1-2). This act of consuming the scroll symbolized the internalization of God's message, making it a part of Ezekiel's very being. It was a powerful representation of the prophet's total commitment to his divine mission, ensuring that his proclamations would be infused with divine truth and authority.

Ezekiel's prophetic messages were not only proclamations of judgment but also contained profound visions of hope and restoration. God's ultimate plan was to bring the Israelites back to Himself, purify them, and restore their land. *"I will give you a new heart and put a new spirit in you; I will remove from you your heart of stone and give you a heart of flesh"* (Ezekiel 36:26). This promise of spiritual renewal was a beacon of hope for the exiled community, assuring them that God's love and mercy would prevail despite their past rebellions.

Ezekiel's calling and vision are a powerful reminder of the transformative impact of encountering God's glory. His experience by the Kebar River was not only a personal commissioning but a pivotal moment that teaches the broader themes of judgment and restoration that would define his prophetic ministry. Ezekiel's unwavering obedience, rooted in his profound vision of God's glory, serves as an enduring example of the power of divine calling and the importance of faithfully delivering God's message, regardless of the challenges faced.

THE NEED FOR RENEWAL

The Israelites in exile were in a state of spiritual desolation. They had turned away from God, worshipped idols, and violated His covenant. Their physical exile mirrored their spiritual condition—disconnected from God and in need of renewal. Ezekiel's prophecies highlighted their need for repentance and a return to faithfulness.

One of the most striking visions in Ezekiel's ministry is the vision of the dry bones in Ezekiel 37. God brought Ezekiel to a valley full of dry bones and asked him, *"Son of man, can these bones live?"* Ezekiel responded, *"Sovereign Lord, you alone know"* (Ezekiel 37:3). God then instructed Ezekiel to prophesy to the bones, telling them to hear the word of the Lord. As he prophesied, there was a rattling sound, and the bones came together, flesh and skin covered them, and breath entered them, bringing them to life.

This vision symbolized the spiritual renewal that God promised to bring to the people of Israel. *"I will put my Spirit in you and you will live, and I will settle you in your own land. Then you will know that I the Lord have spoken, and I have done it, declares the Lord"* (Ezekiel 37:14). The dry bones represented the Israelites' spiritual deadness, and the breath of God symbolized the Holy Spirit bringing new life.

SPIRITUAL REBIRTH

Ezekiel's messages of renewal were not just about physical restoration but also about spiritual rebirth. He prophesied about a new heart and a new spirit that God would give to His people. *"I will give you a new heart and put a new spirit in you; I will remove from you your heart of stone and give you a heart of flesh. And I will put my Spirit in you and move you to follow my decrees and be careful to keep my laws"* (Ezekiel 36:26-27). This promise of transformation was a powerful declaration of God's intention to renew His people from the inside out.

Spiritual rebirth involves a fundamental change in our hearts and minds. It means allowing God to remove our hardened hearts and replace them with hearts that are responsive to His Spirit. This transformation is essential for living a life that honors God and reflects His character. When Ezekiel spoke of hearts of stone being replaced with hearts of flesh, he illustrated the profound

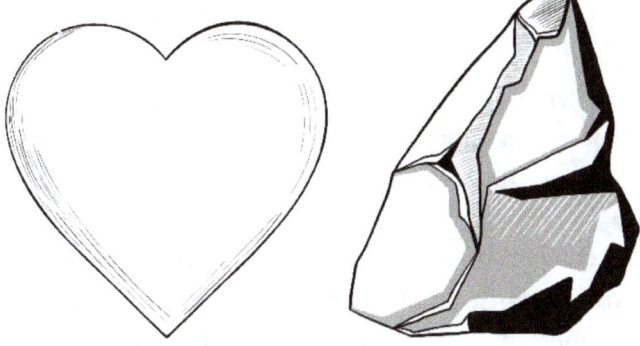

internal change required for true spiritual vitality. A heart of stone symbolizes a state of insensitivity and rebellion against God, whereas a heart of flesh is tender, responsive, and attuned to God's will.

Ezekiel's prophecy emphasizes that this transformation is not something we can achieve on our own; it is a work of God's Spirit within us. The infusion of a new spirit and God's own Spirit into His people signify a complete renewal of their inner being. This divine intervention empowers believers to live according to God's statutes and ordinances, not out of mere obligation, but from a place of genuine desire and commitment. The new spirit represents a renewed mind, aligned with God's purposes, leading to a life that naturally produces righteousness and obedience.

The concept of spiritual rebirth is foundational to the Christian faith. It parallels Jesus' teachings in the New Testament, where He speaks to Nicodemus about the necessity of being born again. *"Very truly I tell you, no one can see the kingdom of God unless they are born again"* (John 3:3). This idea of being born again encapsulates the profound inner change that Ezekiel described, where the old self is put away, and a new, Spirit-led life begins. This rebirth is marked by repentance, the acceptance of God's grace, and the ongoing work of the Holy Spirit within us.

Spiritual rebirth also involves a reorientation of our priorities and values. As God transforms our hearts and minds, we begin to see the world through His eyes. Our desires shift from selfish pursuits to a passion for God's kingdom and His righteousness. This change affects every aspect of our lives, from how we treat others to how we make decisions and use our resources. It cultivates a life of compassion, justice, and love, reflecting God's character in our daily actions.

Ezekiel's vision of spiritual rebirth offers profound hope. For the Israelites in exile, it promised a future where their relationship with God would be restored and revitalized. For us today, it assures us that no matter how far we have strayed or how hardened our hearts have become, God can renew us. His Spirit is powerful enough to transform even the most resistant hearts, making them vessels of His love and grace.

Spiritual rebirth is an ongoing process. It begins with a decisive moment of surrender to God, but it continues as we daily yield to the Holy Spirit's work in our lives. Sanctification, the process of becoming more like Christ, involves continually allowing God to shape our hearts and minds. This ongoing transformation leads to a deeper intimacy with God and a more profound understanding of His will.

Living in the reality of spiritual rebirth means embracing the identity that God gives us as His renewed and beloved children. It means trusting that His Spirit within us is greater than our weaknesses and failures. As we walk in this newness of life, we become living testimonies of God's power to change hearts and lives. We carry the message of hope and renewal to a world in desperate need of God's transformative touch.

Ezekiel's prophecy about spiritual rebirth is a powerful reminder of God's desire to renew us completely. By allowing Him to transform our hearts of stone into hearts of flesh, we open ourselves to a life led by His Spirit, marked by obedience, love, and righteousness. This spiritual renewal not only changes us but also equips us to be agents of God's transformative power in the world around us.

THE TEMPLE VISION

Ezekiel's vision of the new temple in chapters 40-48 is another significant aspect of his prophetic ministry. This detailed vision of a restored temple and the return of God's glory to Israel symbolized the ultimate restoration of God's presence among His people. The vision included precise measurements of the temple, intricate descriptions of its chambers and courtyards, and the glorious return of the Lord's presence to the temple.

"Then the man brought me to the gate facing east, and I saw the glory of the God of Israel coming from the east.

His voice was like the roar of rushing waters, and the land was radiant with his glory" (Ezekiel 43:1-2). This vision offered hope to the exiled Israelites that God's presence would once again dwell among them, and it pointed to a future where God's people would be fully restored in their relationship with Him. The return of God's glory, depicted with such awe-inspiring imagery, reassured the Israelites that despite their current separation and suffering, a time of divine restoration and communion was promised.

Ezekiel's temple vision conveyed more than just physical reconstruction; it represented spiritual renewal and the reestablishment of a sacred space where God and His people could commune. The detailed measurements and specifications highlight the perfection and orderliness of God's plan, reflecting His meticulous care for His dwelling place among His people. Every aspect of the temple was designed to glorify God and facilitate pure, reverent worship.

The vision's emphasis on the return of God's glory teaches the importance of divine presence. For the Israelites, the temple was not merely a physical structure but a symbol of God's abiding presence and covenantal faithfulness. Ezekiel's prophecy rekindled hope that God had not abandoned them despite their exile and sin. The anticipated return of His glory signified that their relationship with Him could be restored, reaffirming their identity as His chosen people.

This vision also serves as a powerful reminder of the importance of worship and reverence for God. The temple was the center of Israelite worship, a place where sacrifices were offered, prayers were lifted, and God's laws were taught. Ezekiel's detailed depiction of the temple's design and function emphasized that worship should be conducted with utmost respect and adherence to God's commandments. It called the people to revere God's holiness and to prioritize their relationship with Him above all else.

In a broader theological context, the temple vision also points to the eschatological hope of a new creation where God's presence will dwell permanently among His people. It foreshadows the ultimate fulfillment of God's promise in Revelation, where John describes a new heaven and a new earth with no need for a temple because the Lord God Almighty and the Lamb are its temple. *"And I heard a loud voice from the throne saying, 'Look! God's dwelling place is now among the people, and he will dwell with them. They will be his people, and God himself will be with them and be their God'"* (Revelation 21:3).

For us as contemporary believers, Ezekiel's vision of the temple calls us to reflect on the centrality of God's presence in our lives. It encourages us to create sacred spaces in our hearts and communities where God's glory can dwell. This involves living in a manner that honors God, dedicating time for worship, prayer, and studying His

Word. It also means fostering an environment of reverence and holiness, where God's presence is welcomed and cherished.

The temple vision also challenges us to evaluate our worship practices. Are they aligned with God's standards, marked by reverence, and focused on His glory? It reminds us that worship is not just a ritual but a heartfelt expression of our relationship with God. True worship engages our entire being and aligns us with God's purposes, transforming us and drawing us closer to Him.

Ezekiel's vision of the new temple is a profound declaration of God's promise to restore His presence among His people. It symbolizes spiritual renewal, emphasizes the importance of worship and reverence, and points to the ultimate fulfillment of God's plan in the new creation. As we reflect on this vision, we are invited to prioritize God's presence in our lives, cultivate a spirit of true worship, and look forward with hope to the day when we will dwell with Him eternally.

RENEWAL THROUGH OBEDIENCE

Ezekiel's life and ministry show the importance of obedience in experiencing renewal and rebirth. His faithful delivery of God's messages, even when they were difficult and met with resistance, exemplifies the kind of obedience that God desires from us. Renewal often requires us to turn away from our old ways and embrace the path that God has set before us.

In Ezekiel 18, God emphasizes personal responsibility and the need for repentance. *"But if a wicked person turns away from all the sins they have committed and keeps all my decrees and does what is just and right, that person will surely live; they will not die"* (Ezekiel 18:21). This passage highlights the transformative power of repentance and obedience. It is never too late to turn back to God and experience His renewal.

EMBRACING GOD'S PROMISE OF RENEWAL

Just as Ezekiel prophesied renewal for the Israelites, we too are offered renewal through our relationship with God. Whether we feel spiritually dry, disconnected, or in need of a fresh start, God promises to renew us through His Spirit. Embracing this promise involves seeking God wholeheartedly and allowing His Spirit to work in us.

"He saved us through the washing of rebirth and renewal by the Holy Spirit, whom he poured out on us generously through Jesus Christ our Savior" (Titus 3:5-6). This New Testament passage echoes Ezekiel's promise of a new heart and spirit, emphasizing that our renewal comes through the Holy Spirit given to us through Jesus Christ.

PRACTICAL STEPS FOR EXPERIENCING RENEWAL

To experience spiritual renewal, we can take practical steps that align us with God's transformative work:

1. **Seek God's Presence:** Spend time in prayer and worship, inviting God's presence into your life. Create space for Him to speak and move.

2. **Confess and Repent:** Acknowledge any areas of sin or disobedience in your life. Confess them to God and ask for His forgiveness and cleansing.

3. **Immerse in Scripture:** Engage with God's Word regularly. Let the truths of Scripture renew your mind and transform your heart.

4. **Listen to the Holy Spirit:** Be attentive to the promptings of the Holy Spirit. Follow His guidance and be open to the changes He wants to make in your life.

5. **Engage in Community:** Surround yourself with a community of believers who can support and encourage you in your journey of renewal. Share your experiences and grow together.

LIVING OUT RENEWAL

Experiencing spiritual renewal is not a one-time event but a continuous journey. As we allow God to renew us, we are called to live out that renewal in our daily lives. This involves embodying the fruits of the Spirit, such as love, joy, peace, patience, kindness, goodness, faithfulness, gentleness, and self-control (Galatians 5:22-23).

Living out renewal also means being a vessel of renewal for others. Just as Ezekiel brought messages of hope and restoration to the Israelites, we too can encourage and uplift those around us. By sharing our testimonies of God's renewing work in our lives, we can inspire others to seek their own renewal.

THE HOPE OF FUTURE RENEWAL

Ezekiel's visions not only provided immediate hope for the exiled Israelites but also pointed to the ultimate renewal that would come through Jesus Christ and the establishment of God's eternal kingdom. This future renewal includes the promise of new heavens and a new earth, where God's presence will dwell fully with His people.

"And I heard a loud voice from the throne saying, 'Look! God's dwelling place is now among the people, and he will dwell with them. They will be his people, and God

himself will be with them and be their God. He will wipe every tear from their eyes. There will be no more death or mourning or crying or pain, for the old order of things has passed away'" (Revelation 21:3-4). This vision of ultimate renewal gives us hope and assurance as we navigate the challenges of this life.

EMBRACING RENEWAL IN EVERY SEASON

No matter what season of life we are in, God's promise of renewal is always available to us. Whether we are experiencing a time of spiritual dryness, facing difficult circumstances, or seeking a fresh start, we can turn to God for renewal and rebirth.

Reflect on areas in your life where you need renewal. Ask God to breathe new life into those areas and to transform your heart and mind. Trust that He is faithful to His promises and that His Spirit is at work within you.

A PRAYER FOR RENEWAL AND REBIRTH

Let us conclude this chapter with a prayer, seeking God's renewal and rebirth in our lives. May we be inspired by Ezekiel's vision and strengthened by God's promises.

Heavenly Father, we thank You for the life and ministry of Ezekiel, who brought messages of renewal and hope to Your people. We ask for Your Spirit to renew us today. Give us new hearts and minds that are responsive to Your leading. Transform us from the inside out and fill us with Your presence. Breathe new life into every area of our lives and help us to live out Your renewal daily. May we be vessels of Your hope and restoration to those around us. In Jesus' name, Amen.

As we continue our journey through the lives of the prophets, let the story of Ezekiel inspire us to seek God's renewal and to embrace the new life He offers. May we be encouraged to live out our faith with a renewed spirit, trusting in God's transformative power and His promises of a glorious future.

VISION – YOUR GRANDFATHER IS GOING HOME

My grandfather and grandmother took great efforts to give my sister and myself the best opportunities they could afford.

I remember them taking us to The Tweetsie Railroad at Blowing Rock, N.C. For many summers, we packed a bag lunch and headed for this park. It was so much fun riding the train.

Grandfather also taught us to drive. He took us on the farm and we drove in the fields.

He taught us to work. We helped him with the cattle and the sheep.

And often he said, "Money does not grow on trees."

One summer, I was taking a two- week course at Wake Forest. It just so happened that my grandfather was placed in a hospital close by. He was suffering from heart failure.

A couple of days before he died, The Holy Spirit visited me in a comforting manner.

I had gone on a walk, and suddenly The Holy Spirit appeared. A bright shadow hung over my head. The shining light poured upon me. Then I heard a heavenly voice.

"Your grandfather is going home."

I knew that The Holy Spirit was preparing me for his death.

The next day, I went back to the hospital. He could barely speak, but he grabbed my hand. He wanted me to tell him about everyone in the family. I assured him that everyone was doing well, and was concerned for him.

After he heard that all the family members were fine, he slipped into a peaceful sleep.

I left the hospital, and went to my room to study. As I was studying, a **luminous shadow** swept through the room, and went out the window. I knew that his spirit had just departed.

I called the hospital, and was informed that he had passed away at the moment that the **luminous shadow** swept through my room!

"But when he, the Spirit of truth, comes, he will guide you into all the truth. He will not speak on his own; he will speak only what he hears, and he will tell you what is yet to come." (John 16:13)

REFLECTION QUESTIONS

1. Reflecting on Ezekiel's initial vision of God's glory, how do you seek and respond to God's presence in your life? Are there specific ways you can create more space to experience His presence and hear His voice?

2. Ezekiel prophesied about God giving a new heart and spirit. Are there areas in your life where you feel spiritually dry or disconnected? How can you invite the Holy Spirit to renew and transform your heart?

3. Ezekiel's obedience was crucial to his prophetic ministry. In what ways is God calling you to be obedient in your life? How might this obedience lead to spiritual renewal and a deeper relationship with Him?

4. How can you actively live out the renewal you experience in your daily life? What practical steps can you take to embody the fruits of the Spirit and be a source of renewal for others around you?

5. Ezekiel's visions pointed to an ultimate renewal and restoration through Jesus Christ. How does this promise of future restoration influence your current outlook on life's challenges? How can you keep this eternal perspective in mind as you navigate your daily struggles and decisions?

7

DANIEL - WISDOM AND PROTECTION

Daniel, a beacon of faith and wisdom during the Babylonian exile, stands out as a remarkable example of steadfastness and divine insight. His life, marked by unwavering devotion to God in a foreign and often hostile land, offers profound lessons on the power of prayer, wisdom, and divine protection. From interpreting dreams for kings to surviving the lions' den, Daniel's experiences highlight the extraordinary impact of living a life fully committed to God's guidance and wisdom.

Daniel's prophecies and visions reveal God's sovereignty over the kingdoms of the earth and His ultimate plan for redemption and restoration. His story encourages us to seek God's wisdom in all circumstances and to trust in His protection, no matter how formidable the challenges we face. As we explore the life and ministry of Daniel, we are inspired to cultivate a deeper relationship with God, characterized by faithfulness, prayer, and a reliance on His divine wisdom and protection. Through Daniel's example, we learn that living a life aligned with God's will enables us to navigate life's complexities with confidence and grace, knowing that God is always in control.

DANIEL'S WISDOM IN EXILE

Daniel was among the young men taken into Babylonian captivity during the reign of King Nebuchadnezzar. Despite being in a foreign land and surrounded by pagan influences, Daniel remained true to his faith. His commitment to God was evident from the very beginning, as he refused to defile himself with the king's food and wine, opting instead for a diet of vegetables and water. This act of obedience, though seemingly small, set the tone for Daniel's life of unwavering faith and divine wisdom.

"But Daniel resolved not to defile himself with the royal food and wine, and he asked the chief official for permission not to defile himself this way" (Daniel 1:8). God honored Daniel's commitment, granting him and his friends better health than those who ate the royal food. This initial act of faithfulness demonstrated Daniel's reliance on God's wisdom and set the stage for the extraordinary events that would follow.

One of the most notable aspects of Daniel's life was his God-given ability to interpret dreams and visions. This gift not only distinguished him from others but also played a crucial role in the Babylonian court. When King Nebuchadnezzar had a troubling dream that none of his wise men could interpret, Daniel sought God's wisdom through prayer.

"During the night the mystery was revealed to Daniel in a vision. Then Daniel praised the God of heaven and said: 'Praise be to the name of God for ever and ever; wisdom and power are his. He changes times and seasons; he deposes kings and raises up others. He gives wisdom to the wise and knowledge to the discerning. He reveals deep and hidden things; he knows what lies in darkness, and light dwells with him'" (Daniel 2:19-22).

Daniel's ability to interpret the king's dream not only saved his life and the lives of his friends but also elevated him to a position of high honor in the kingdom. This event teaches us the importance of seeking God's wisdom in all situations. When faced with challenges that seem insurmountable, turning to God for guidance can lead to remarkable outcomes.

PROTECTION IN THE LION'S DEN

Perhaps the most well-known story of Daniel's life is his miraculous protection in the lion's den. Under King

Darius, Daniel's consistent practice of praying to God three times a day led to his entrapment by jealous officials. These officials, envious of Daniel's favor with the king and his impeccable integrity, devised a scheme to undermine him. They convinced King Darius to issue a decree that prohibited prayer to any god or human other than the king for thirty days, knowing that Daniel would not comply. The decree, sealed with the irrevocable law of the Medes and Persians, was intended to create an impossible situation for Daniel.

Despite the decree, Daniel continued his practice of prayer, demonstrating his unwavering faith and courage. *"Now when Daniel learned that the decree had been published, he went home to his upstairs room where the windows opened toward Jerusalem. Three times a day he got down on his knees and prayed, giving thanks to his God, just as he had done before"* (Daniel 6:10). Daniel's actions reflect a deep commitment to his faith, showing that his relationship with God was more important than his own safety. He did not hide his devotion or modify his practices out of fear, but instead, he boldly continued to worship God openly.

This defiance led to Daniel being thrown into the lion's den, a punishment designed to ensure a gruesome death. The den was a sealed pit filled with hungry lions, meant to be an inescapable death sentence. Yet, in this moment of extreme peril, God's protection was miraculously evident. *"My God sent his angel, and he shut the mouths of the lions. They have not hurt me, because I was found innocent in his sight. Nor have I ever done any wrong before you, Your Majesty"* (Daniel 6:22). This divine intervention not only saved Daniel's life but also demonstrated God's sovereign power over creation.

The angelic intervention in the lion's den is a powerful testament to God's ability to protect those who are faithful to Him. The shutting of the lions' mouths symbolizes God's control over the forces of nature and His commitment to safeguard His servants. Daniel's experience serves as a profound reminder that God is with us in the most dangerous and dire circumstances, providing protection and deliverance in ways that transcend human understanding.

King Darius, witnessing this miracle, was deeply moved and issued a decree honoring the God of Daniel. *"I issue a decree that in every part of my kingdom people must fear and reverence the God of Daniel. For he is the living God and he endures forever; his kingdom will not be destroyed, his dominion will never end"* (Daniel 6:26). This turn of events highlights the broader impact of Daniel's faithfulness: it not only preserved his life but also led to a powerful testimony of God's greatness before the entire kingdom. Daniel's ordeal and subsequent deliverance became a catalyst for proclaiming God's sovereignty to a pagan nation.

The story of Daniel in the lion's den teaches us several key lessons about faith, courage, and divine protection. Firstly, it highlights the importance of maintaining our spiritual disciplines and commitments, even when faced with severe consequences. Daniel's example shows us that our relationship with God must take precedence over all else, and that true faith requires steadfastness in the face of adversity.

Secondly, the story illustrates that God's protection is not limited by human constraints. While Daniel's situation seemed hopeless from a human perspective, God intervened in a miraculous way. This reassures us that no matter how desperate our circumstances, God's power to save and protect is boundless. Our faithfulness to God invites His miraculous intervention and opens the door for His glory to be revealed.

Finally, Daniel's experience in the lion's den serves as an encouragement that our trials can lead to greater testimony and witness for God. Through his unwavering faith and God's miraculous deliverance, Daniel became a powerful witness to the living God. His story inspires us to trust in God's protection and to remain faithful, knowing that our experiences can serve to strengthen the faith of others and proclaim God's power and goodness.

Despite the seemingly inevitable death, Daniel's faith remained steadfast. He was not alone in the den; God sent an angel to shut the mouths of the lions, protecting Daniel from harm. The next morning, King Darius hurried to the den and called out to Daniel, who responded that God had sent His angel to save him because he was found innocent in God's sight (Daniel 6:21-22). This miraculous deliverance not only saved Daniel but also led King Darius to issue a decree that all people must fear and reverence the God of Daniel, recognizing His power and sovereignty.

DANIEL 10 – GABRIEL FIGHTS AGAINST THE PRINCE OF PERSIA

In Daniel 10, we find a fascinating glimpse into the spiritual realm and the cosmic battles that occur beyond our physical sight. Daniel had been fasting and praying for three weeks when he received a vision of a heavenly being. This being, identified as the angel Gabriel in later chapters, explained that he had been delayed by the "prince of the Persian kingdom," a demonic force opposing God's purposes.

Gabriel's struggle with this prince lasted for twenty-one days until Michael, one of the chief princes, came to assist him. This passage highlights the reality of spiritual warfare and the battles that angels fight on behalf of God's people. It reassures us that our prayers are heard and that heavenly forces are at work, even when we do not see immediate results. Daniel's experience encourages us to remain persistent in prayer, trusting that God is moving and that His angels are engaged in battles on our behalf.

HOW WISDOM HELPS US PRAY

Wisdom plays a crucial role in enhancing our prayer lives, guiding us to pray in ways that align with God's will and His purposes. Proverbs 2:6 tells us, *"For the Lord gives wisdom; from His mouth come knowledge and understanding."* When we seek God's wisdom, we are better equipped to understand His desires and to intercede effectively.

Wisdom helps us discern what to pray for and how to pray. It allows us to recognize the deeper needs beneath surface issues and to ask for God's guidance and intervention in specific and meaningful ways. James 1:5 encourages us to ask for wisdom if we lack it, assuring us that God gives generously to all without finding fault. By incorporating wisdom into our prayers, we align ourselves more closely with God's heart and His plans, making our prayers more powerful and effective.

Furthermore, wisdom helps us approach prayer with the right attitude. It teaches us humility, recognizing that we are dependent on God's insight and direction. It also fosters patience, understanding that God's timing and answers are perfect, even when they differ from our expectations. As we grow in wisdom, our prayers become a reflection of a mature faith, characterized by trust in God's sovereignty and His unfailing love.

THE ROLE OF PRAYER IN SEEKING WISDOM AND PROTECTION

Daniel's life highlights the critical role of prayer in seeking divine wisdom and protection. Throughout his life, Daniel consistently turned to God in prayer, whether he was seeking understanding of dreams, facing imminent danger, or interceding for his people. His prayer life was a source of strength and guidance, enabling him to navigate the challenges of exile with grace and wisdom.

In Daniel 9, we see a profound example of his intercessory prayer for the restoration of Jerusalem. *"So I turned to the Lord God and pleaded with him in prayer and petition, in fasting, and in sackcloth and ashes. I prayed to the Lord my God and confessed: 'Lord, the great and awesome God, who keeps his covenant of love with those who love him and keep his commandments, we have sinned and done wrong'"* (Daniel 9:3-5). Daniel's heartfelt prayer demonstrated his deep concern for his people and his reliance on God's mercy and guidance.

PRACTICAL STEPS FOR SEEKING WISDOM AND PROTECTION

To seek wisdom and protection in our own lives, we can follow the example set by Daniel. Here are some practical steps:

1. **Commit to Regular Prayer:** Establish a consistent prayer routine. Set aside specific times each day to seek God's wisdom and protection, just as Daniel did.

2. **Seek God's Guidance in All Decisions:** Before making decisions, big or small, seek God's wisdom. Ask for His insight and understanding to guide your choices.

3. **Study God's Word:** Immerse yourself in Scripture to gain wisdom and discernment. The Bible is a rich source of guidance for every aspect of life.

4. **Trust in God's Protection:** When facing challenges or dangers, trust that God is with you. Remember His promises of protection and rely on His strength.

5. **Intercede for Others:** Pray for the needs of others, just as Daniel interceded for his people.

Your prayers can have a powerful impact on the lives of those around you.

DIVINE PROTECTION IN TIMES OF CRISIS

Daniel's experience in the lion's den is a powerful reminder of God's protection in times of crisis. While most of us may never face literal lions, we encounter metaphorical lions in the form of trials, fears, and dangers. Daniel's story encourages us to trust in God's ability to protect us, no matter the circumstances.

The story of Daniel's friends—Shadrach, Meshach, and Abednego—also illustrates divine protection. When they refused to bow down to the golden image set up by King Nebuchadnezzar, they were thrown into a blazing furnace. Yet, God delivered them without a single burn. *"Then King Nebuchadnezzar leaped to his feet in amazement and asked his advisers, 'Weren't there three men that we tied up and threw into the fire?' They replied, 'Certainly, Your Majesty.' He said, 'Look! I see four men walking around in the fire, unbound and unharmed, and the fourth looks like a son of the gods'"* (Daniel 3:24-25).

Both stories remind us that God's protection is not limited by our circumstances. Whether we are in a den of lions or a blazing furnace, God's presence is with us, safeguarding us from harm.

WISDOM IN NAVIGATING LIFE'S CHALLENGES

The wisdom that Daniel exhibited throughout his life is another key lesson for us. His ability to interpret dreams, provide wise counsel to kings, and navigate complex political situations was rooted in his deep relationship with God. This wisdom was not his own but was given to him by God in response to his faithfulness and prayer.

In Daniel 2:20-21, Daniel acknowledges the source of his wisdom: *"Praise be to the name of God for ever and ever; wisdom and power are his. He changes times and seasons; he deposes kings and raises up others. He gives wisdom to the wise and knowledge to the discerning."* Recognizing that true wisdom comes from God, we too can seek His guidance to navigate the complexities of our lives.

To cultivate wisdom, we must prioritize our relationship with God. Spending time in His presence, studying His Word, and seeking His guidance in prayer are essential practices. Additionally, surrounding ourselves with wise and godly counsel can provide valuable insights and help us grow in discernment

THE ROLE OF ANGELS IN PROTECTION

Daniel's encounters with angels highlight the role of divine messengers in offering protection and guidance.

In Daniel 10, we read about a vision in which the angel Gabriel explains a spiritual battle happening behind the scenes. *"But the prince of the Persian kingdom resisted me twenty-one days. Then Michael, one of the chief princes, came to help me, because I was detained there with the king of Persia"* (Daniel 10:13). This passage reveals the reality of spiritual warfare and the role of angels in protecting and assisting God's people.

Understanding the role of angels can deepen our awareness of God's provision and care for us. While we may not always be aware of their presence, we can trust that God's angels are at work, providing protection and guidance according to His will.

LIVING WITH CONFIDENCE IN GOD'S WISDOM AND PROTECTION

Living with confidence in God's wisdom and protection means trusting Him in every aspect of our lives. It involves seeking His guidance in our decisions, relying on His protection in times of danger, and maintaining a steadfast faith even when circumstances are challenging.

Daniel's life is a powerful example of what it means to live with this kind of confidence. His unwavering commitment to prayer, his trust in God's wisdom, and his reliance on divine protection enabled him to navigate the trials of exile with grace and strength.

As we reflect on Daniel's story, let us be encouraged to deepen our own commitment to seeking God's wisdom and protection. By cultivating a vibrant prayer life, immersing ourselves in Scripture, and trusting in God's presence, we can face life's challenges with confidence and peace.

A PRAYER FOR WISDOM AND PROTECTION

Let us conclude this chapter with a prayer, seeking God's wisdom and protection in our lives. May we be inspired by Daniel's example and strengthened by God's promises.

Heavenly Father, we thank You for the life and example of Daniel, who demonstrated unwavering faith and reliance on Your wisdom and protection. We ask for Your wisdom to guide us in all our decisions and Your protection to shield us from harm. Help us to remain steadfast in our commitment to prayer and to trust in Your presence, no matter the challenges we face. May we live with confidence in Your promises, knowing that You are with us always. In Jesus' name, Amen.

As we continue our journey through the lives of the prophets, let the story of Daniel inspire us to seek God's wisdom and to trust in His protection. May we be encouraged to live out our faith with confidence, relying on God's guidance and safeguarding in every aspect of our lives.

DEMONIC SPIRITS – WISDOM TO DEAL WITH THEM

I have been blessed to sense angels, to briefly see angels, and to hear a choir of angels singing. However, I have also encountered demonic spirits. Such experiences occurred suddenly, and I needed instant wisdom.

One day I had an encounter with a demonic – oppressed person. This happened on the job, which made it even more difficult. I had to use wisdom and maintain my composure.

I felt like Daniel in the lion's den. He was thrown into a deadly situation. Likewise, I was commanded to meet a certain person in a room.

I should have insisted that another person be present.

Immediately, the person slammed the door, and came face -to-face with me. She lashed out with loud and ugly words. The screaming was so loud that I thought my ears might burst. I took a step back to protect myself.

Then, without warning, her eyes rolled back inside her head. Her face contorted. A glazed look covered her eyes. Her voice changed to the pitch of a man. Her upper body started jerking back and forth.

I sat still in silence and prayed quietly. I had been around wounded animals, and I knew not to make any sudden moves.

Unless, heaven intervened, I would be struck. I prayed that an angel would protect me from this demon.

To this day, I do not know what incidence triggered this demonic rage.

Then Divine Intervention happened. Someone knocked on the door, and I heard people in the hall.

She heard the knock on the door, and responded. Her eyes rolled back into place, and she answered the door. I did not need any ques; I walked out the door.

The Holy Spirit helped me keep my composure and wait. Wisdom taught me to never enter a room alone with anyone on the job.

REFLECTION QUESTIONS

1. How can you incorporate the discipline of regular prayer, like Daniel, into your daily routine? What steps can you take to ensure that your commitment to God remains steadfast, even in challenging situations?

2. In what areas of your life do you need to seek God's wisdom more actively? Reflect on a recent decision or situation where you could have benefited from seeking divine guidance before acting.

3. Consider a time when you felt vulnerable or faced a significant challenge. How did you experience God's protection, and how can Daniel's story of protection in the lion's den encourage you to trust in God's safeguarding presence in your life today?

4. Daniel's unwavering faith had a profound impact on those around him, including King Darius. How can your faithfulness to God and your commitment to prayer and righteousness influence and inspire others in your community or workplace?

5. Daniel's experiences highlight the role of angels in providing protection and guidance. How does understanding the presence and role of angels in your life affect your confidence in God's constant care and intervention?

8

HOSEA - LOVE AND REDEMPTION

Hosea, one of the most genuine and heartfelt prophets, offers a vivid portrayal of God's relentless love and the power of redemption. His life and ministry, marked by the unique and challenging call to marry Gomer, a woman prone to unfaithfulness, serve as a profound allegory for God's unwavering love for His wayward people. Hosea's personal experiences mirror the spiritual adultery of Israel, highlighting God's enduring commitment to reclaim and restore His people despite their repeated betrayals.

The prophecies of Hosea are filled with themes of love, mercy, and redemption, reflecting God's deep sorrow over Israel's unfaithfulness and His unyielding desire to bring them back to Himself. Through Hosea's story, we witness the depth of God's love that pursues us even when we stray, offering us hope and a path to reconciliation. As we explore the life and messages of Hosea, we are reminded of the transformative power of God's love and the boundless mercy He extends to us. Hosea's narrative

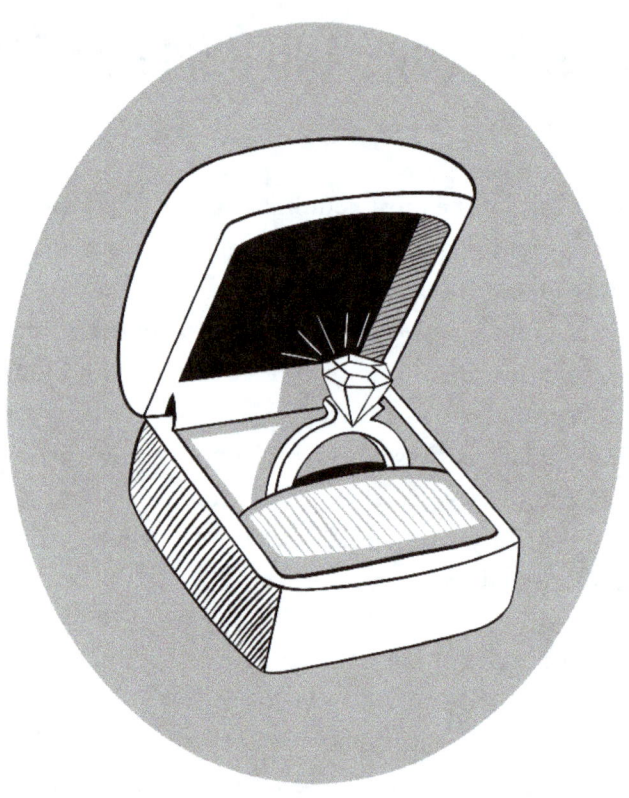

encourages us to embrace God's redemptive love, trust in His promises, and extend the same grace and forgiveness to others in our lives.

HOSEA'S CALL AND MARRIAGE

Hosea's prophetic journey began with a personal and challenging call from God. He was instructed to marry Gomer, a woman known for her promiscuity. This command was not just a test of Hosea's obedience but also a symbolic act representing God's relationship with Israel. *"When the Lord began to speak through Hosea, the Lord said to him, 'Go, marry a promiscuous woman and have children with her, for like an adulterous wife this land is guilty of unfaithfulness to the Lord'"* (Hosea 1:2).

Hosea's marriage to Gomer mirrored Israel's unfaithfulness to God. Just as Gomer was unfaithful to Hosea, Israel had turned away from God, pursuing other gods and breaking the covenant. Despite Gomer's infidelity, Hosea's persistent love and commitment to her reflected God's steadfast love for His people.

THE PAIN OF UNFAITHFULNESS

Hosea's relationship with Gomer was marked by pain and betrayal, yet it was also a powerful illustration of God's enduring love. Gomer's unfaithfulness and the

subsequent birth of children with symbolic names—
Jezreel (representing judgment), Lo-Ruhamah (not
loved), and Lo-Ammi (not my people)—highlighted
the consequences of Israel's spiritual adultery.

*"The Lord said to Hosea, 'Call him Lo-Ammi (which
means 'not my people'), for you are not my people, and I
am not your God'"* (Hosea 1:9). These names conveyed
a stark message about the broken relationship between
God and Israel. Yet, even in the midst of judgment,
God's love shone through, pointing to a future hope of
reconciliation and restoration.

GOD'S RELENTLESS LOVE

One of the most striking aspects of Hosea's story is the
depiction of God's relentless love. Despite Israel's repeated unfaithfulness, God's love for His people never
wavered. This love is beautifully expressed in Hosea 2:14-
23, where God speaks of wooing Israel back to Himself,
turning the Valley of Trouble into a door of hope.

*"Therefore I am now going to allure her; I will lead her
into the wilderness and speak tenderly to her. There I
will give her back her vineyards and will make the Valley
of Achor a door of hope"* (Hosea 2:14-15). This passage
highlights God's desire to restore His relationship with
His people, transforming their places of trouble into
opportunities for renewal.

God's love is further illustrated in Hosea 11, where He reflects on His relationship with Israel as a father to a child. *"When Israel was a child, I loved him, and out of Egypt I called my son. But the more they were called, the more they went away from me... How can I give you up, Ephraim? How can I hand you over, Israel?... My heart is changed within me; all my compassion is aroused"* (Hosea 11:1-8). These verses convey the depth of God's compassion and His unwillingness to give up on His people.

THE POWER OF REDEMPTION

Hosea's life also highlights the power of redemption. In Hosea 3, God instructs Hosea to go and love Gomer again, despite her unfaithfulness. Hosea's act of redeeming Gomer from a life of harlotry and bringing her back home symbolizes God's redemptive love for Israel.

"The Lord said to me, 'Go, show your love to your wife again, though she is loved by another man and is an adulteress. Love her as the Lord loves the Israelites, though they turn to other gods and love the sacred raisin cakes.' So I bought her for fifteen shekels of silver and about a homer and a lethek of barley" (Hosea 3:1-2). Hosea's redemption of Gomer is a powerful metaphor for God's willingness to pay any price to restore His people to Himself.

This act of redemption speaks volumes about God's love for us. No matter how far we stray, God's love reaches out to bring us back, offering forgiveness and a new beginning. It reminds us that our worth is not diminished by our failures; instead, God's love redeems and restores us to a place of honor.

EMBRACING GOD'S REDEMPTIVE LOVE

Understanding and embracing God's redemptive love is crucial for our spiritual growth. God's love is not conditional on our behavior; it is a steadfast and unchanging love that seeks to restore us even when we fall short. Embracing this love involves accepting God's forgiveness and allowing His love to transform our hearts and lives.

"But God demonstrates his own love for us in this: While we were still sinners, Christ died for us" (Romans 5:8). This New Testament passage echoes the message of Hosea, highlighting that God's love for us is demonstrated through the ultimate act of redemption—Jesus' sacrifice on the cross.

LIVING OUT GOD'S LOVE

Embracing God's redemptive love also calls us to live out that love in our relationships with others. Just as Hosea loved and redeemed Gomer, we are called to extend grace and forgiveness to those around us. This involves showing compassion, offering second chances, and loving others unconditionally.

Living out God's love can be challenging, especially when we encounter betrayal or hurt. However, Hosea's story encourages us to love beyond the limits of human capacity, relying on God's strength to extend grace. By doing so, we reflect God's love to the world and become agents of His redemptive work.

PRAYING FOR LOVE AND REDEMPTION

Prophetic prayer can be a powerful tool for seeking God's love and redemption in our lives and relationships. When we pray for love and redemption, we invite God to heal our hearts, restore broken relationships, and transform our communities with His love.

One way to pray for love and redemption is to ask God to reveal any areas in our lives where we need His healing touch. We can pray for the grace to forgive others, the strength to love unconditionally, and the courage to seek reconciliation. Additionally, we can intercede for others, asking God to bring His redemptive love into their lives and circumstances.

PRACTICAL STEPS FOR EMBRACING LOVE AND REDEMPTION

To embrace God's love and experience His redemption, we can take practical steps that align us with His heart:

1. **Reflect on God's Love:** Spend time meditating on scriptures that speak of God's love and redemption. Let these truths sink deeply into your heart and mind.

2. **Accept Forgiveness:** Acknowledge your need for God's forgiveness and receive it with gratitude. Allow His love to cleanse and renew you.

3. **Extend Grace:** Practice extending grace and forgiveness to others. Recognize that just as you have been forgiven, you are called to forgive.

4. **Seek Reconciliation:** Take steps to reconcile broken relationships. Reach out to those you have wronged or who have wronged you, seeking to restore peace.

5. **Demonstrate Love:** Actively look for ways to demonstrate God's love in your daily life. This can be through acts of kindness, words of encouragement, or simply being present for others.

THE TRANSFORMATIVE POWER OF REDEMPTION

Hosea's story teaches us about the transformative power of redemption. God's love has the ability to change hearts, restore relationships, and bring new life. When we experience God's redemption, we are not only forgiven but also transformed into new creations.

"Therefore, if anyone is in Christ, the new creation has come: The old has gone, the new is here!" (2 Corinthians 5:17). This verse highlights the complete transformation that occurs through Christ's redemptive work. Embracing this transformation means letting go of our past and stepping into the new life that God offers.

Living as new creations involves allowing God's love to shape our identity and actions. It means seeing ourselves as beloved children of God and living out that identity in our relationships and choices. It also means continually seeking God's presence and guidance, allowing His Spirit to lead us in every aspect of our lives.

A PRAYER FOR LOVE AND REDEMPTION

Let us conclude this chapter with a prayer, seeking God's love and redemption in our lives. May we be inspired by Hosea's example and strengthened by God's promises.

Heavenly Father, we thank You for the life and ministry of Hosea, who demonstrated Your relentless love and the power of redemption. We ask for Your love to fill our hearts and transform our lives. Help us to accept Your forgiveness and extend grace to others. Heal our broken relationships and restore us to a place of honor in Your kingdom. May we live as new creations, reflecting Your love and bringing hope to those around us. In Jesus' name, Amen.

As we continue our journey through the lives of the prophets, let the story of Hosea inspire us to embrace God's love and redemption. May we be encouraged to live out our faith with a renewed understanding of God's unwavering love and His desire to restore and transform us.

I WANT YOU

Love is the essence of Jesus Christ. Scripture even states that people will know that we are His disciples, if we show love for one another. In other words, we should treat people with love.

"One of them, the disciple whom Jesus loved, was reclining next to him." (John 13:23)

During my early days of prayer ministry, I often struggled with a question in my mind. And only the Holy Spirit could know that this was a concern for me!

I had been raised in a church that does not promote women preachers. It was a wonderful church to learn about salvation. And God's Word was taught with great respect.

And even when I took on some roles as a prayer leader, I often wondered how significant my leadership could become.

One weekend, my husband and I attended a Holy Spirit meeting at Richmond, Virginia. I went to the meeting with the desire to hear a word from The Holy Spirit.

We both enjoyed the teaching sessions. While the sessions were great, I still had no clear direction from the Holy Spirit.

The evening session was coming to a close, and soon we would be leaving.

My heart was so hungry for an encounter with the Holy Spirit. I made several sacrifices to be here.

All eyes were bowed for the closing prayer. But I did not hear the speaker pray.

Instead, a heavenly voice spoke directly to my spirit. The voice was so loud that I wondered if others could hear it.

"I Want You," Those words were not spoken by a person. They were relayed by the Holy Spirit.

I was so excited. God wanted me. He wanted me to be on His team. Regardless of what others thought, God wanted me.

A HOME FOR SPRINKLES

Yes, I love pets. Pets have brought joy and healing to my family. I know the value of pets. When I worked in a Nursing Home, Pet Therapy was very important.

Every week, volunteers would bring loving pets. They would go from room to room and allow the residents to pet them. I saw residents laugh, cry and sing after petting these animals.

Included in this chapter are pictures of the cat named Sprinkles.

Sprinkles did not have a loving family. He was in an animal shelter with other cats. But he was such a special cat. He wanted a home. My husband went to this shelter and found Sprinkles. This cat gravitated towards my husband. They connected.

When Sprinkles arrived at my son's house, he was so happy. He lavished all the love and hugs. He gobbled his food, and played with the cat toys. He was so happy to have a home.

The pictures of Sprinkles demonstrate his joy. And Sprinkles returns love to the family.

He poises himself in the most flashing positions. He wants to show his love.

I remember a time when little Sprinkles got lost. For hours we looked for him. Finally, I turned to Cole. He is a jet- black cat, with shining eyes. Cole is a very smart cat.

I looked at Cole. Then I said, "Show me where to find Sprinkles." He stood up and walked towards the living room. He stopped at a chair and lifted his paw. He also stared at the chair. And there was little Sprinkles. He had got caught in the chair!

Love is indeed the greatest virtue. (I Corinthians 13) Our prayers should be as streams of passion flowing from a heart of love towards our Savior!

REFLECTION QUESTIONS

1. How does Hosea's story help you comprehend the depth of God's love for you, even when you stray? Reflect on a time when you experienced God's relentless love in your life despite your own shortcomings.

2. Hosea extended grace and forgiveness to Gomer despite her unfaithfulness. Are there areas in your life where you need to accept God's forgiveness or extend forgiveness to others? What steps can you take to embrace and offer grace?

3. Hosea's obedience to God's challenging call to marry Gomer illustrates his deep commitment. How do you respond when God calls you to difficult tasks? What can you learn from Hosea's example about obedience and trust?

4. Hosea's act of redeeming Gomer symbolizes God's redemptive love for us. How can you live out this redemption in your daily life? Consider ways you can demonstrate God's love and forgiveness in your relationships and interactions.

5. Reflect on how prophetic prayer can play a role in seeking love and redemption in your life.

How can you incorporate prayers for healing, reconciliation, and transformation into your spiritual practices to align more closely with God's redemptive work?

9

JONAH - OBEDIENCE AND MERCY

Jonah, the reluctant prophet, offers a compelling narrative about obedience and God's boundless mercy. His story is unique among the prophetic books, not just for its adventurous elements but for the profound lessons it imparts about God's compassion for all people, even those outside of Israel. Called to deliver a message of repentance to the wicked city of Nineveh, Jonah's initial reaction was to flee, showcasing the human tendency to resist divine assignments when they challenge our prejudices and fears.

The book of Jonah is a powerful reminder of God's relentless pursuit and mercy. Despite Jonah's disobedience and his attempt to escape God's call, God provided a dramatic means of correction and salvation through a great fish. Jonah's eventual obedience led to the repentance of Nineveh, demonstrating that no one is beyond the reach of God's grace. As we explore Jonah's journey, we are encouraged to examine our own responsiveness to God's call and to extend His mercy to those we might deem undeserving. Jonah's story teaches us that God's love and compassion know no bounds and that our obedience can lead to profound transformations, both in our lives and in the lives of others.

JONAH'S CALL AND REBELLION

Jonah's prophetic mission began with a clear and direct call from God. *"The word of the Lord came to Jonah son of Amittai: 'Go to the great city of Nineveh and preach against it, because its wickedness has come up before me'"* (Jonah 1:1-2). Unlike other prophets who eagerly accepted their divine assignments, Jonah's response was one of outright rebellion. Instead of heading to Nineveh, Jonah boarded a ship bound for Tarshish, attempting to flee from God's presence.

Jonah's decision to flee highlights the human tendency to resist God's call when it seems daunting or uncomfortable. His actions show us the struggle between our own desires and God's will. However, Jonah's story also demonstrates that running from God is futile; His purposes will ultimately prevail.

THE STORM AND THE GREAT FISH

Jonah's attempt to escape God's call led to a dramatic encounter at sea. As he sailed away from Nineveh, a violent storm threatened to destroy the ship. The sailors, recognizing the supernatural nature of the storm, cast lots to determine the cause of their peril, and the lot fell on Jonah. When confronted, Jonah confessed his disobedience and instructed the sailors to throw him overboard to calm the storm.

"Pick me up and throw me into the sea," he replied, *"and it will become calm. I know that it is my fault that this great storm has come upon you"* (Jonah 1:12). Jonah's willingness to sacrifice himself to save the sailors demonstrated a moment of humility and responsibility for his actions. However, this was not the end of his story. As Jonah was cast into the sea, he was swallowed by a great fish, appointed by God to save him from drowning.

PROPHETIC SIGNIFICANCE OF 3 DAYS IN THE BELLY OF A WHALE AND JESUS IN THE EARTH

The story of Jonah being in the belly of a whale for three days and three nights holds profound prophetic significance, especially when paralleled with Jesus' death and resurrection. In the book of Jonah, we read that Jonah was swallowed by a great fish and remained in its belly for three days and nights after he attempted to flee from God's command to prophesy to the city of Nineveh (Jonah 1:17). This period was a time of intense reflection, repentance, and renewal for Jonah, culminating in his eventual obedience to God's call.

This event foreshadows the death, burial, and resurrection of Jesus Christ. Jesus Himself made this connection explicit when He said, *"For as Jonah was three days and three nights in the belly of a huge fish, so the Son of Man will be three days and three nights in the heart of the earth"* (Matthew 12:40). Just as Jonah's time in the fish was a precursor to his mission of bringing repentance to Nineveh, Jesus' time in the grave preceded His resurrection, which brings salvation and new life to all who believe.

The three days symbolize a period of transformation and divine intervention. For Jonah, it was a journey from disobedience to alignment with God's will. For Jesus, it was the transition from death to victory over sin and death, affirming His identity as the Messiah and Savior. This prophetic parallel emphasizes the themes of redemption, obedience, and the fulfillment of God's purposes.

The story of Jonah and the resurrection of Jesus both highlight God's mercy and willingness to save. Jonah's deliverance from the whale led to the repentance of Nineveh, showcasing God's compassion even for those outside of Israel. Similarly, Jesus' resurrection offers hope and salvation to all humanity, extending God's grace to every corner of the earth.

The three days in the belly of the whale and Jesus' three days in the earth serve as powerful symbols of God's redemptive plan, underscoring His ability to bring life out of death, hope out of despair, and obedience out of reluctance. These events call us to reflect on our own need for repentance and to embrace the new life offered through Christ's resurrection.

A PRAYER OF REPENTANCE

Inside the belly of the fish, Jonah experienced a profound moment of repentance and renewal. In his darkest hour, he turned to God in prayer, acknowledging his need for divine intervention. *"In my distress I called to the Lord, and he answered me. From deep in the realm of the dead I called for help, and you listened to my cry"* (Jonah 2:2).

Jonah's prayer from within the fish is a powerful example of how turning to God in repentance can lead to restoration. Despite his initial disobedience, Jonah's heartfelt plea for mercy was heard by God, who commanded the fish to vomit Jonah onto dry land. This act of divine mercy illustrates God's readiness to forgive and restore those who turn back to Him.

OBEDIENCE AND PROCLAMATION

After his miraculous deliverance, Jonah received a second call from God to go to Nineveh. This time, he obeyed. *"Then the word of the Lord came to Jonah a second time: 'Go to the great city of Nineveh and proclaim to it the message I give you.' Jonah obeyed the word of the Lord and went to Nineveh"* (Jonah 3:1-3). Jonah's eventual obedience shows the importance of following God's directives, even after initial reluctance.

Upon arriving in Nineveh, Jonah proclaimed God's message of impending judgment: *"Forty more days and Nineveh will be overthrown"* (Jonah 3:4). Despite his reluctance, Jonah's message was effective. The people of Nineveh, from the greatest to the least, believed God, declared a fast, and put on sackcloth as a sign of repentance. Even the king of Nineveh humbled himself, decreeing that everyone should call urgently on God and give up their evil ways.

GOD'S MERCY ON NINEVEH

The repentance of Nineveh moved God to show mercy. *"When God saw what they did and how they turned from their evil ways, he relented and did not bring on them the destruction he had threatened"* (Jonah 3:10). This act of mercy displays God's compassionate nature and His desire for all people to turn from their sins and be saved. The story of Nineveh's repentance highlights that no one is beyond the reach of God's grace, and His mercy triumphs over judgment.

JONAH'S ANGER AND GOD'S LESSON

Despite the incredible turnaround in Nineveh, Jonah was displeased and angry that God had shown mercy. *"But to Jonah this seemed very wrong, and he became angry. He prayed to the Lord, 'Isn't this what I said, Lord, when I was still at home? That is what I tried to forestall by fleeing to Tarshish. I knew that you are a gracious and compassionate God, slow to anger and abounding in love, a God who relents from sending calamity'"* (Jonah 4:1-2).

Jonah's reaction reveals a struggle that many of us face: the tension between wanting justice for others and accepting God's mercy. To teach Jonah a lesson, God caused a plant to grow and provide shade for him, only to wither the next day. When Jonah expressed his anger over the plant's demise, God challenged him: *"You have been concerned about this plant, though you did not tend it or make it grow. It sprang up overnight and died overnight. And should I not have concern for the great city of Nineveh, in which there are more than a hundred and twenty thousand people who cannot tell their right hand from their left—and also many animals?"* (Jonah 4:10-11).

Through this object lesson, God emphasized the value of compassion and the importance of His mercy extending to all, even those whom we may deem undeserving.

EMBRACING OBEDIENCE AND MERCY

Jonah's story calls us to embrace both obedience to God's call and the extension of His mercy to others. Obedience involves trusting God's wisdom and following His directions, even when they lead us into uncomfortable or challenging situations. It means setting aside our personal biases and desires to fulfill God's purposes.

Similarly, extending mercy requires us to reflect God's compassionate nature. Just as God showed mercy to the people of Nineveh, we are called to show mercy to those around us. This involves forgiving others, offering second chances, and recognizing that everyone is in need of God's grace.

PRAYING FOR OBEDIENCE AND MERCY

Prophetic prayer can help us cultivate obedience and mercy in our lives. When we pray for obedience, we ask God to align our hearts with His will, to give us the courage to follow His directives, and to help us overcome our resistance. Praying for mercy involves seeking God's compassion for ourselves and others, asking for the ability to forgive, and interceding for those who need God's grace.

PRACTICAL STEPS FOR CULTIVATING OBEDIENCE AND MERCY

To cultivate obedience and mercy, we can take practical steps that help us align our lives with God's purposes:

1. **Reflect on God's Call:** Spend time in prayer and meditation, seeking clarity on what God is calling you to do. Be open to His guidance, even if it challenges your comfort zone.

2. **Practice Immediate Obedience:** When you sense God directing you, respond without delay. Trust that His plans are good and that He will provide the strength you need.

3. **Extend Forgiveness:** Make a conscious effort to forgive those who have wronged you. Recognize that forgiveness is a gift of grace, reflecting the mercy that God has shown you.

4. **Show Compassion:** Look for opportunities to demonstrate compassion and mercy in your daily interactions. Whether through acts of kindness, words of encouragement, or support for those in need, let God's love shine through you.

5. **Intercede for Others:** Pray regularly for those who are struggling, those who need to

experience God's mercy, and those whom God has placed on your heart. Your prayers can have a powerful impact on their lives.

THE TRANSFORMATIVE POWER OF OBEDIENCE AND MERCY

Jonah's story teaches us about the transformative power of obedience and mercy. When we obey God's call, we open the door for His purposes to be fulfilled in our lives and the lives of others. Similarly, when we extend mercy, we participate in God's redemptive work, bringing healing and restoration to those around us.

"For I desire mercy, not sacrifice, and acknowledgment of God rather than burnt offerings" (Hosea 6:6). This verse highlights the importance of mercy in our relationship with God and others. God values a heart that is compassionate and merciful, more than religious rituals and sacrifices.

LIVING OUT OBEDIENCE AND MERCY

Living out obedience and mercy involves a daily commitment to follow God's lead and to show His love to others. It requires humility, willingness to be transformed, and a deep reliance on God's grace. By embracing these qualities, we become more like Christ and reflect His character in the world.

A PRAYER FOR OBEDIENCE AND MERCY

Let us conclude this chapter with a prayer, seeking God's guidance for obedience and His heart for mercy. May we be inspired by Jonah's story and strengthened by God's promises.

Heavenly Father, we thank You for the life and lessons of Jonah. Help us to embrace obedience to Your call, even when it challenges us. Give us the courage to follow Your directions and the humility to submit to Your will. Fill our hearts with Your mercy, so that we may extend forgiveness and compassion to others. Transform us by Your grace and use us to bring Your love and redemption to those around us. In Jesus' name, Amen.

Let the story of Jonah inspire us to respond to God's call with obedience and to extend His mercy to others. May we be encouraged to live out our faith with a renewed understanding of God's desires and His boundless compassion.

A GLIMPSE OF THE COURTS IN HEAVEN

This chapter about Jonah, the prophet, portrays the importance of obeying God's instructions. The Holy Spirit will give us clear directions, if we ask and receive. The Holy Spirit will never ask us to do anything contrary to God's Word.

At one point, I was considering changing careers. But I did not have an inner peace about it. I began to pray about this concern and the answer came in an unusual manner!

A couple of years before the COVID-19 pandemic, I witnessed a scene from heaven. Yes, I had been praying about the career change, but did not expect to see such a compelling vision.

As I was pondering my choices, a scene from heaven suddenly appeared. I saw a heavenly spirit, standing up before a judge, in a courtroom setting. This heavenly spirit was defending me. I understood that the heavenly being was pleading for me and my family. The heavenly spirit was speaking to the judge, and he held up his right arm.

I remember seeing that right arm. I watched as he spoke to the judge. Then, the heavenly being turned around and looked at me. One word came out of his mouth. This word was, "destruction."

There was no mistake. He did say, "Destruction." At this point, I realized that if I made this change, I might place my family in a path of destruction in the future.

It is always easier to look back. If I had changed careers, I would have been working in a high-risk environment for COVID-19. My family would also be in danger.

After seeing this heavenly courtroom scene, I was not reluctant. Without hesitation, I stayed with my current job. I am so grateful that I obeyed the Holy Spirit in this matter.

REFLECTION QUESTIONS

1. Reflect on a time when you felt God calling you to do something difficult or uncomfortable. How did you respond, and what did you learn from that experience about obedience and trust?

2. How has God shown you mercy in your own life, especially in times when you may have strayed from His will? How can remembering these moments help you extend mercy to others?

3. Jonah initially fled from God's call, which led to a series of challenging events. When you face challenges or resistance in following God's direction, how can you find the courage to persevere and obey?

4. Jonah struggled with accepting God's mercy towards Nineveh. Are there people or groups in your life that you find difficult to show compassion and mercy to? How can you work on extending God's love and grace to them?

5. Jonah's prayer in the belly of the fish was a turning point for him. How can you incorporate heartfelt prayers of repentance and renewal into your spiritual practice, especially when you realize you have been resistant to God's call?

10

MALACHI - FAITHFULNESS AND COVENANT

Malachi, the final prophet of the Old Testament, brings a poignant and challenging message of faithfulness and covenant. His ministry came at a time when the Israelites had returned from exile and rebuilt the temple, yet their hearts had grown cold and their worship had become routine and insincere. Malachi's words are a powerful call to return to genuine devotion, highlighting the importance of honoring God with sincere worship, integrity, and faithful stewardship.

Malachi's prophecies address the people's neglect and unfaithfulness in various aspects of their covenant relationship with God, including their offerings, their marriages, and their overall commitment to God's commands. Through Malachi, God passionately appeals to His people to return to Him, promising that His blessings will follow genuine repentance and faithful living. As we explore the messages of Malachi, we are reminded of the critical importance of living out our faith with authenticity and integrity. His calls for renewal and the promise of the coming "messenger" who will prepare the way for the Lord resonate deeply, urging us to examine our own faithfulness and commitment to God. Malachi's story encourages us to uphold our covenant with God, trusting in His unwavering love and readiness to restore those who earnestly seek Him.

MALACHI'S CALL TO A FAITHFUL COVENANT

Malachi's ministry occurred during a time when the people of Israel had returned from Babylonian exile and rebuilt the temple in Jerusalem. Despite their physical return, their spiritual condition remained in need of restoration. The people's commitment to God had waned, and their worship had become routine and insincere. Malachi's messages were direct and confrontational, addressing the various ways the Israelites had been unfaithful to their covenant with God.

Malachi begins his message by affirming God's love for Israel, reminding them of their special relationship with Him. *"I have loved you," says the Lord. But you ask, 'How have you loved us?'"* (Malachi 1:2). This foundational statement teaches the basis of the covenant—God's unwavering love for His people. Despite their unfaithfulness, God's love remained constant, and He sought to restore the relationship.

HONOR AND REVERENCE FOR GOD

One of the primary issues Malachi addresses is the lack of honor and reverence for God among the priests and the people. The priests, who were responsible for leading the people in worship, had become complacent and careless in their duties. They offered blemished and substandard sacrifices, violating the requirements of the law and showing disrespect to God.

"A son honors his father, and a slave his master. If I am a father, where is the honor due me? If I am a master, where is the respect due me?' says the Lord Almighty. 'It is you priests who show contempt for my name. But you ask, 'How have we shown contempt for your name?' By offering defiled food on my altar'" (Malachi 1:6-7). This passage highlights the importance of approaching God with the honor and reverence He deserves. Our worship should be sincere and reflective of our love and respect for Him.

FAITHFULNESS IN MARRIAGE AND RELATIONSHIPS

Malachi also addresses the issue of unfaithfulness in marriage, highlighting the significance of honoring the covenant of marriage. He condemns the practice of divorce and the mistreatment of spouses, emphasizing that marriage is a sacred covenant established by God.

"The man who hates and divorces his wife,' says the Lord, the God of Israel, 'does violence to the one he should protect,' says the Lord Almighty. So be on your guard, and do not be unfaithful" (Malachi 2:16). This call to faithfulness extends beyond the marital relationship to all aspects of our interactions with others. God desires that we treat each other with love, respect, and integrity, reflecting His character in our relationships.

TITHES AND OFFERINGS

Another key area of faithfulness that Malachi addresses is the practice of tithes and offerings. The Israelites had neglected their financial obligations to God, withholding the tithes that were meant to support the temple and the Levites. This lack of faithfulness in giving was seen as robbing God and failing to honor Him with their resources.

"Will a mere mortal rob God? Yet you rob me. But you ask, 'How are we robbing you?' In tithes and offerings. You are under a curse—your whole nation—because you are robbing me" (Malachi 3:8-9). Malachi calls the people to bring the full tithe into the storehouse, promising that God will bless them abundantly in return. *"Bring the whole tithe into the storehouse, that there may be food in my house. Test me in this,' says the Lord Almighty, 'and see if I will not throw open the floodgates of heaven and pour out so much blessing that there will not be room enough to store it"* (Malachi 3:10).

THE COMING OF THE MESSENGER

One of the most significant prophecies in the book of Malachi is the promise of the coming messenger who will prepare the way for the Lord. This prophecy points to John the Baptist, who would later prepare the way for Jesus Christ.

"I will send my messenger, who will prepare the way before me. Then suddenly the Lord you are seeking will come to his temple; the messenger of the covenant, whom you desire, will come,' says the Lord Almighty" (Malachi 3:1). This announcement not only provided hope for the future but also called the people to prepare their hearts and lives for the coming of the Lord.

THE DAY OF THE LORD

Malachi concludes his message with a focus on the coming Day of the Lord, a day of judgment and purification. He warns of the consequences of continued unfaithfulness and calls the people to return to God with sincerity and repentance.

"Surely the day is coming; it will burn like a furnace. All the arrogant and every evildoer will be stubble, and the day that is coming will set them on fire,' says the Lord Almighty. 'Not a root or a branch will be left to them. But for you who revere my name, the sun of righteousness will rise

with healing in its rays. And you will go out and frolic like well-fed calves" (Malachi 4:1-2). This powerful imagery contrasts the fate of the wicked with the blessings for those who honor God, offering both a warning and a promise of hope.

EMBRACING FAITHFULNESS IN OUR LIVES

Malachi's call to faithfulness is as relevant today as it was in his time. Our relationship with God is based on a covenant of love and commitment, and we are called to honor that covenant with sincerity and devotion. Embracing faithfulness involves several key aspects:

1. **Honor and Reverence for God:** Approach God with the respect and honor He deserves. Ensure that your worship is sincere and reflective of your love for Him.

2. **Faithfulness in Relationships:** Honor your commitments in marriage and treat others with love, respect, and integrity. Reflect God's character in all your interactions.

3. **Faithfulness in Giving:** Honor God with your resources by giving faithfully and generously. Recognize that everything you have comes from Him and respond with gratitude and trust.

4. **Preparation for the Lord:** Keep your heart and life prepared for the Lord's coming. Live in a way that reflects your anticipation of His return and your commitment to His kingdom.

PRAYING FOR FAITHFULNESS AND COVENANT

Prophetic prayer can help us cultivate faithfulness and honor our covenant relationship with God. When we pray for faithfulness, we ask God to strengthen our commitment to Him, to help us honor our promises, and to live in a way that pleases Him. Praying for covenant involves seeking God's guidance in our relationships, our worship, and our stewardship of resources.

PRACTICAL STEPS FOR CULTIVATING FAITHFULNESS AND COVENANT

To cultivate faithfulness and honor our covenant with God, we can take practical steps that align our lives with His desires:

1. **Daily Devotion:** Spend time each day in prayer and scripture reading. Let God's Word shape your thoughts, actions, and priorities.

2. **Reflect on Your Commitments:** Regularly evaluate your commitments to God and others.

Make adjustments as needed to ensure that you are honoring your promises.

3. **Practice Generosity:** Be intentional about giving to God's work and to those in need. Trust that God will provide for you as you honor Him with your resources.

4. **Prepare for the Lord:** Live with an awareness of Christ's return. Let this anticipation influence your decisions, actions, and attitudes.

5. **Seek Accountability:** Surround yourself with a community of believers who can support and encourage you in your journey of faithfulness. Share your struggles and victories with others who can walk alongside you.

THE TRANSFORMATIVE POWER OF FAITHFULNESS

Malachi's message teaches us about the transformative power of faithfulness. When we honor our covenant with God, we experience His blessings and favor. Our relationship with Him deepens, and our lives reflect His love and grace. Faithfulness transforms not only our individual lives but also our communities and the world around us.

"He has shown you, O mortal, what is good. And what does the Lord require of you? To act justly and to love mercy

and to walk humbly with your God" (Micah 6:8). This verse encapsulates the essence of faithfulness—acting justly, loving mercy, and walking humbly with God. When we embrace these qualities, we fulfill our covenant relationship with God and become conduits of His love and justice in the world.

Living out faithfulness and honoring our covenant with God involves a daily commitment to follow His lead and to show His love to others. It requires humility, willingness to be transformed, and a deep reliance on God's grace. By embracing these qualities, we become more like Christ and reflect His character in the world.

MALACHI 4 – HEALING IN HIS WINGS

The final chapter of the Old Testament, Malachi 4, contains a powerful and hopeful prophecy about the coming day of the Lord. One of the most beautiful and profound promises in this chapter is found in verse 2, where Malachi speaks of the "sun of righteousness" rising with "healing in its wings."

"But for you who revere my name, the sun of righteousness will rise with healing in its wings. And you will go out and frolic like well-fed calves." (Malachi 4:2)

This imagery of the sun rising with healing in its wings paints a vivid picture of hope and restoration. The "sun of righteousness" is often interpreted as a metaphor for the Messiah, Jesus Christ, who brings light, life, and healing to a world overshadowed by sin and darkness. Just as the dawn breaks and dispels the night, the coming of Christ brings the light of God's righteousness and the promise of spiritual and physical healing.

The phrase "healing in its wings" evokes the image of the rays of the sun spreading out like wings, bringing warmth and restoration to all they touch. In ancient times, wings were also a symbol of protection and care, much like a bird sheltering its young. This dual imagery underscores the comprehensive nature of the healing that Christ brings—covering every aspect of our lives and providing both physical and spiritual renewal.

For the people of Malachi's time, who were experiencing spiritual apathy and disillusionment, this promise was a beacon of hope. It assured them that despite the current hardships and unfaithfulness, God's ultimate plan included a future where righteousness would prevail and healing would come.

For us today, this prophecy is a reminder of the healing power of Christ in our lives. Whether we are facing physical ailments, emotional wounds, or spiritual brokenness, we can find solace in the promise that Jesus, the sun of righteousness, rises with healing in His wings. His light dispels the darkness of our lives, bringing restoration and wholeness.

This passage also encourages us to revere God's name and live in anticipation of His healing touch. It invites us to trust in His promises and to look forward to the day when all things will be made new. The joy and freedom depicted—going out and frolicking like well-fed calves—reflect the abundant life that comes from living under the care and protection of our Messiah.

A PRAYER FOR FAITHFULNESS AND COVENANT

Let us conclude this chapter with a prayer, seeking God's guidance for faithfulness and His strength to honor our covenant with Him. May we be inspired by Malachi's message and strengthened by God's promises.

Heavenly Father, we thank You for the life and lessons of Malachi. Help us to embrace faithfulness to Your covenant and to honor You in all aspects of our lives. Strengthen our commitment to You and guide us in our relationships, our worship, and our stewardship of resources. Fill our hearts with a sincere love for You and a desire to live in a way that pleases You. May we reflect Your character in our interactions with others and prepare our hearts for the coming of the Lord. In Jesus' name, Amen.

Let the story of Malachi inspire us to remain faithful to God and to honor our covenant relationship with Him. May we be encouraged to live out our faith with a renewed understanding of God's desires and His unwavering love.

THE COVENANT AND THE CAR

A majority of my prayer time, consists of praying scriptures from The Bible. God's Word is a true foundation for my faith. His promises are so precious.

"Where is the wise person? Where is the teacher of the law? Where is the philosopher of this age? Has not God made foolish the wisdom of the world?" (I Corinthians 1:20)

Jesus encouraged us to ask for our needs to be met, and struggles to be resolved.

"You may ask me for anything in my name, and I will do it." (John 14: 14)

When I was in my early thirties, I longed for a new car. I had driven second hand cars for a long time. And all too often, these second- hand cars needed repairs.

Finally, I realized that if I were to ever own a new car, I would have to pray for it.

I asked the Holy Spirit to show me how to pray for a new car. In response to my request, a scripture came to mind.

"Now faith is confidence in what we hope for and assurance about what we do not see." (Hebrews 11:1)

Several times when I prayed this scripture, I saw (in the spirit), a title deed to a car. Also, I received instructions from the Holy Spirit.

I walked two to three miles most every day. There was a car lot with new cars just about a mile from my house. Day after day, I walked to this car lot and prayed. I walked around the new cars and prayed for the title deed to a new car.

MAZDA 323

In addition to praying consistently for a new car with a title deed, I saved money. It seemed that God's Spirit helped me to save money. Each month, I put money into a special "car fund."

One day, I saw the car that I wanted. It was a maroon Mazda 323. Maybe you can remember this model. It had a very high rating, and it had plenty of room for us.

The car dealer saw me looking at the car, and invited me to the office to discuss the details. We started signing the papers, then he suddenly stated that I did not have enough credit to buy the car. This was because I was young, and had paid for most everything I owned. Despite this setback, I did not give up. I showed the dealer the money that I had saved. ($6000) That got his attention. I was able to pay about two-thirds of the cost of the car.

Suddenly, he forgot all about the credit and sold me the car. This car was a great vehicle. It was reliable and did not need many repairs.

Over, 270,000 miles were put on that car, and it was still running smoothly. At that point, we gave the car to a family member. And it served him well.

Truly, God is faithful. As the mountains stand tall and sure, God is true to His Word!

REFLECTION QUESTIONS

1. How can you ensure that your worship is sincere and not just a routine? Reflect on ways to cultivate a deeper, more authentic relationship with God in your daily practices.

2. In what ways can you demonstrate greater faithfulness and integrity in your relationships? Consider both your marriage, if applicable, and your interactions with others. How can you reflect God's love and commitment in these relationships?

3. Malachi addresses the importance of tithes and offerings. How can you better honor God with your resources? Reflect on your current practices of giving and consider ways to be more generous and faithful with what God has entrusted to you.

4. What steps can you take to live in constant readiness for the Lord's return? How can this anticipation influence your daily decisions and actions to align more closely with God's will?

5. Reflect on the aspects of your life where you can more fully embrace and live out the covenant relationship with God. How can you act justly, love mercy, and walk humbly with God in practical and meaningful ways?

11

WOMEN PROPHETS

Throughout God's Word, women have played pivotal roles in the unfolding story of redemption and revelation. The lives and ministries of women prophets highlight their significant contributions to God's work among His people. These women, through their faithfulness, courage, and prophetic voices, remind us of the diverse ways God can speak and act through individuals, regardless of gender. This chapter explores the lives of several notable women prophets and the impact they had on their communities and the broader narrative of Scripture.

ANNA (LUKE 2:36-38)

Anna, a prophetess mentioned in the Gospel of Luke, provides a beautiful example of faithfulness and devotion. Luke describes her as the daughter of Phanuel, of the tribe of Asher, and she was very old, having lived with her husband seven years after her marriage and then as a widow until she was eighty-four. Anna never left the temple but worshiped night and day, fasting and praying.

When Jesus was presented at the temple, Anna gave thanks to God and spoke about the child to all who were looking forward to the redemption of Jerusalem. Anna's life of dedicated worship and her recognition of Jesus as the Messiah highlights the importance of spiritual vigilance and the role of prophetic insight in pointing others toward God's redemptive work.

ISAIAH'S WIFE (ISAIAH 8:3)

Isaiah's wife is another significant yet often overlooked prophetess. Referred to simply as "the prophetess" in Isaiah 8:3, she bore a son whose name was divinely chosen to convey a prophetic message to the people of Israel. The naming of their son, Maher-Shalal-Hash-Baz, meaning "quick to the plunder, swift to the spoil," served as a living prophecy of the impending Assyrian invasion and the swift judgment that would come upon Israel and Syria.

Though the details of her life and ministry are sparse, Isaiah's wife played a crucial role in the prophetic ministry shared with her husband. Her example reminds us that the prophetic ministry often involves both speaking and embodying God's messages, sometimes through the very names and lives of one's children.

DEBORAH (JUDGES)

Deborah stands out as one of the most prominent female leaders and prophets in the Bible. Described as a prophetess and judge, she led Israel during a tumultuous time. Deborah held court under the Palm of Deborah, where the Israelites came to her to have their disputes decided. Her leadership was marked by wisdom, courage, and an unwavering commitment to God's commands.

In Judges 4, Deborah's prophetic role is highlighted when she calls Barak to lead an army against the oppressive Canaanite king Jabin and his commander, Sisera. Despite Barak's hesitation, Deborah's faith in God's promise led to a decisive victory for Israel. After the battle, Deborah and Barak sang a song of praise to God, celebrating His deliverance. Deborah's story illustrates the power of faith and obedience and demonstrates that God can raise leaders from unexpected places to accomplish His purposes.

HULDAH (2 CHRONICLES 34:21-33)

Huldah, a prophetess during the reign of King Josiah, played a pivotal role in one of the most significant religious reforms in Israel's history. When the Book of the Law was discovered in the temple, Josiah sent his officials to consult Huldah. Her response confirmed that the book was indeed the word of the Lord and pronounced judgment on the nation for their disobedience.

However, Huldah also conveyed a message of hope. Because Josiah had humbled himself before God, the disaster foretold would not occur during his lifetime. Huldah's prophecy spurred Josiah to renew the covenant, leading to widespread religious reform and a return to the worship of the Lord. Huldah's story underscores the importance of seeking God's guidance through His prophets and highlights the significant influence a woman's prophetic voice can have on the spiritual direction of a nation.

MIRIAM (EXODUS 15:20; MICAH 6:4)

Miriam, the sister of Moses and Aaron, is recognized as a prophetess in the Old Testament. Her role in Israel's history is significant, beginning with her watchful care over Moses as an infant and continuing through the Exodus from Egypt. After the miraculous crossing of the Red Sea, Miriam led the women of Israel in song and dance, praising God for His deliverance.

"Then Miriam the prophet, Aaron's sister, took a timbrel in her hand, and all the women followed her, with timbrels and dancing. Miriam sang to them: 'Sing to the Lord, for he is highly exalted. Both horse and driver he has hurled into the sea.'" (Exodus 15:20-21).

Miriam's prophetic ministry, however, was not without its challenges. In Numbers 12, she and Aaron spoke against Moses, leading to her temporary affliction with leprosy as a consequence. Despite this, Miriam is remembered as one of the key leaders who helped guide Israel out of slavery. Her legacy is a testament to the enduring impact of faithful leadership and worship, even amid human imperfections.

PHILIP'S DAUGHTERS (ACTS 21:9)

In the New Testament, we find mention of Philip the evangelist's four unmarried daughters who prophesied. Though their individual prophecies are not recorded, their inclusion in the Acts of the Apostles highlights the presence and acceptance of female prophetic voices in the early Christian community.

"He had four unmarried daughters who prophesied" (Acts 21:9).

These women were part of a vibrant and active ministry that played a role in the early church's expansion and spiritual growth. Their prophetic ministry illustrates that the gift of prophecy was not confined to men but was a vital part of the spiritual fabric of the early church, involving women who were committed to serving God and using their gifts for His glory.

THE DAUGHTERS OF ZELOPHEHAD (NUMBERS 27:1-7)

While not prophets in the traditional sense, the daughters of Zelophehad are noteworthy for their bold appeal for justice and their significant impact on Israelite inheritance laws. Mahlah, Noah, Hoglah, Milkah, and Tirzah approached Moses and the leaders of Israel to request an inheritance from their father, who had died without sons. Their request was unprecedented, as inheritance traditionally passed through male descendants.

God affirmed their plea, instructing Moses to grant them their father's inheritance and establishing a legal precedent for future generations. This act of courage and faith not only secured their family's legacy but also demonstrated the importance of advocating for justice within the community of faith.

"So Moses brought their case before the Lord, and the Lord said to him, 'What Zelophehad's daughters are saying is right. You must certainly give them property as an inheritance among their father's relatives and give their father's inheritance to them'" (Numbers 27:5-7).

Their story highlights the role of women in shaping the laws and traditions of Israel and emphasizes the broader theme of God's justice and fairness.

THE IMPACT OF WOMEN PROPHETS

The stories of these women prophets illustrate the diverse ways in which God can use women to convey His messages, lead His people, and effect significant change. Whether through direct prophecy, leadership, or advocacy, these women demonstrated remarkable faith and courage.

Their lives challenge us to recognize and value the contributions of women in ministry and leadership within the faith community. They remind us that God's call transcends gender and that His Spirit equips and empowers all believers to participate in His work.

The lives and ministries of women prophets in the Bible offer rich insights into the ways God works through all people to accomplish His purposes. Their stories inspire us to embrace our own callings with faith and courage, knowing that God's Spirit empowers us to make a significant impact in our communities and the world. As we reflect on their contributions, may we be encouraged to support and uplift one another in our shared mission to honor God and advance His kingdom.

THE VISION OF THE HEAVENLY EAR

During the early days of the prayer ministry, I had a wonderful friend. She had been radically saved, and was devoted to prayer. Several times a week, she came to the church to pray for the church. Many times, she walked the sanctuary alone, praying for the church to flourish, and souls to be saved.

Gifts of prophecy operated through her. She had heavenly visions that were inspiring and confirmed with Scriptures.

Every year, we had a Prayer Team from the Appalachian Conference that attended the National Day of Prayer in Washington D.C. We were invited by the leader of the Capitol Hill Prayer Partners, Sara Ballenger. She is a mighty woman of prayer!

The intercessors began praying for the nation. Such prayers included protection for the nation, and wisdom for our leaders. During the prayer time, I noticed that my friend was not in the group. I looked for her, and saw her sitting by a window. She was deep in prayer. She was praying passionately for the nation. I sat beside her, and asked her what she was seeing in the spirit realm.

"A very large ear from heaven hovered in the clouds over the region. The ear was not a human ear, and it was turned towards the city. It was apparent that the ear was a "spiritual living thing which was engaged in the job of hearing prayers."

Directly above us, a gleaming light shined upwards.

For me it is important to receive confirmation from the Scriptures when such experiences happen. The verse that came to our minds was from Psalm 88:2.

"May my prayer come before you;
turn your ear to my cry."

REFLECTION QUESTIONS

1. How do the stories of women prophets in the Bible challenge your understanding of the roles women can play in ministry and leadership within the faith community?

2. Reflect on the example of Anna and her life of dedicated worship and prayer. How can you cultivate a deeper, more personal relationship with God in your daily life?

3. In what ways can you recognize and encourage the spiritual gifts and leadership abilities of women in your own faith community? What practical steps can you take to support and uplift them?

4. The daughters of Zelophehad advocated for justice within their community. How can you stand up for what is right and seek equitable treatment for all, especially those who may be marginalized or overlooked?

5. Considering the diverse leadership styles of Deborah and Miriam, how can you embrace and promote diverse leadership within your own faith community? What benefits can this bring to your community?

12

THE UNKNOWN PROPHETS

The Bible is filled with stories of well-known prophets who delivered powerful messages from God, but there are also many prophets whose names and stories are less familiar. These "unknown" prophets played crucial roles in God's unfolding plan, often delivering timely messages that spurred action, encouraged faith, and brought about divine intervention. Their stories remind us that prophetic voices are not limited to the famous or celebrated; God can use anyone to speak His truth and bring about His will. This chapter explores the lives of some of these lesser-known prophets and relates their examples to how people today can rise up and pray prophetically.

THE CALL FOR MODERN-DAY PROPHETS

In our world today, there is a great need for prophetic voices—people who are attuned to God's Spirit and willing to speak His truth. These modern-day prophets may not have the public recognition of biblical figures like Isaiah or Jeremiah, but their role is no less significant. They are called to pray fervently, listen attentively to God's voice, and boldly proclaim His messages, even when it is challenging or unpopular.

As believers, we are all called to rise up and pray prophetically. This means seeking God's guidance, interceding for our communities, and being willing to act on the insights and directions He gives us. Just as the unknown prophets of the Bible played pivotal roles in their times, we too can have a profound impact by being faithful to God's call.

JEHOSHAPHAT (2 CHRONICLES 20:20)

Jehoshaphat, the king of Judah, provides a compelling example of the power of believing in God's prophets. Faced with a formidable coalition of enemies, Jehoshaphat called the people of Judah to seek the Lord. As they gathered in prayer and fasting, a prophetic word came through Jahaziel, a Levite, who assured them of God's deliverance.

"Early in the morning they left for the Desert of Tekoa. As they set out, Jehoshaphat stood and said, 'Listen to me, Judah and people of Jerusalem! Have faith in the Lord your God and you will be upheld; have faith in his prophets and you will be successful.'" (2 Chronicles 20:20).

Jehoshaphat's call to believe in God's prophets under-scores the importance of heeding prophetic messages. The faith of the people in God's promise, delivered through His prophet, led to a miraculous victory. They marched into battle with praise and worship, and God caused their enemies to turn on each other. This story illustrates that prosperity and success come when we trust in God's words delivered through His messengers.

THE PROPHET IN 2 CHRONICLES 20:14

In the same narrative, Jahaziel, the prophet, delivered a crucial message before the battle. The Spirit of the Lord came upon him, and he spoke to the assembly:

"Then the Spirit of the Lord came on Jahaziel son of Zechariah, the son of Benaiah, the son of Jeiel, the son of Mattaniah, a Levite and descendant of Asaph, as he stood in the assembly. He said: 'Listen, King Jehoshaphat and all who live in Judah and Jerusalem! This is what the Lord says to you: "Do not be afraid or discouraged because of this vast army. For the battle is not yours, but God's."" (2 Chronicles 20:14-15).

This prophetic word provided reassurance and guid-ance. It reminded the people that the battle belonged to the Lord and that they should not fear. This proph-ecy came at a critical moment, bolstering the faith of the people and giving them the courage to face their enemies. Jahaziel's role highlights how prophetic messages can prepare us for spiritual battles and help us stand firm in God's promises.

GIDEON (JUDGES 6 AND 7)

The story of Gideon is another powerful example of God sending a prophet in response to the cries of His people. The Israelites were suffering under the oppression of the Midianites, and in their distress, they called out to the Lord. God responded by sending a prophet who reminded them of His past deliverances and their current disobedience.

"When the Israelites cried out to the Lord because of Midian, he sent them a prophet, who said, 'This is what the Lord, the God of Israel, says: I brought you up out of Egypt, out of the land of slavery. I rescued you from the hand of the Egyptians. And I delivered you from the hand of all your oppressors. I drove them out before you and gave you their land.'" (Judges 6:7-9).

Following this prophetic message, the angel of the Lord appeared to Gideon, calling him to deliver Israel from the Midianites. Despite his initial hesitation and doubts, Gideon eventually rose to the challenge, leading a small army to victory through God's miraculous intervention. Gideon's story demonstrates that God often prepares and calls ordinary people to accomplish extraordinary feats through prophetic encouragement and divine empowerment.

RELATING TO MODERN-DAY PROPHETS

The stories of these unknown prophets and their significant impacts encourage us to recognize the value of prophetic voices in our own time. God continues to speak through His people today, and we are called to listen, respond, and act on His words.

1. **Seek God's Guidance:** Just as the people of Judah and Gideon sought the Lord in times of crisis, we must continually seek God's guidance through prayer and fasting. By dedicating ourselves to spiritual disciplines, we position ourselves to hear God's voice more clearly and receive His direction.

2. **Trust in Prophetic Messages:** Believing in the words delivered by God's prophets is essential. Jehoshaphat's success came from his faith in God's promise through Jahaziel. When we receive prophetic messages, we should weigh them against Scripture, seek confirmation through prayer, and act in faith.

3. **Prepare for Spiritual Battles:** Prophetic words often come before significant challenges or battles.

Jahaziel's prophecy prepared the people of Judah for victory. Similarly, we should be attentive to prophetic insights that can equip us to face spiritual and practical challenges with confidence.

4. **Respond to God's Call:** Like Gideon, we may feel inadequate or hesitant when God calls us to take on significant tasks. However, God's calling comes with His empowerment. By trusting in His strength and guidance, we can rise to the occasion and fulfill His purposes.

5. **Be a Prophetic Voice:** God can use anyone to deliver His messages. Whether through spoken words, acts of service, or intercessory prayer, we are all called to be prophetic voices in our communities. This involves speaking truth, encouraging faith, and advocating for justice and righteousness.

The stories of the unknown prophets in the Bible remind us that God's messages often come through unexpected and humble servants. Their faithfulness and courage had profound impacts on their communities and the broader narrative of Scripture. Today, we are called to rise up as prophetic voices, seeking God's guidance, trusting in His promises, and responding to His call with faith and obedience. By doing so, we can play a significant role in God's ongoing work of redemption and restoration in our world.

A WELL-OILED MACHINE

We were young and newly married, when we joined a Spirit-Filled Church. This means that the church believes in The Power of the Holy Spirit. The new pastor and his wife wanted to bless all the people in the congregation. So, they asked to visit each household. We agreed for them to visit us and pray for our family.

The pastor and his wife began with a prayer for our family. They prayed for God's protection and provision. They also prayed for our child.

The beautiful presence of the Lord filled the room as they prayed. Then suddenly, the pastor began to prophesy. He laid hands upon me and prayed.

"You will be like a well-oiled machine." (I understood this to be in matters of family and ministry).

He also prophesied the following:

"You will have divine connections in your life."

These words greatly encouraged me. I was inspired to seek the Lord more diligently.

After, 20 years of ministry, I see that these words have been fulfilled.

I have been involved in prayer ministries for our nation, our churches, our regions, and even individuals. I have led NIGHT WATCH prayers. I have also led prayers at the National Day of Pray.

Yes, these words by an unknown prophet, compelled me towards the ministry of prayer!

REFLECTION QUESTIONS

1. How can you cultivate the habit of seeking God's guidance through prayer and fasting in your daily life, similar to how the people of Judah and Gideon did in times of crisis?

2. Reflect on a time when you received a message or insight that you felt was from God. How did you respond, and what steps did you take to confirm and act on that message?

3. Think about a significant challenge or "battle" you are currently facing. How can you prepare spiritually for this challenge by seeking prophetic insights and relying on God's promises?

4. Have you ever felt inadequate or hesitant when faced with a task or calling from God, like Gideon? How can you trust in God's empowerment and guidance to overcome these feelings and fulfill His purposes?

5. In what ways can you be a prophetic voice in your community? Consider how you can speak truth, encourage faith, and advocate for justice and righteousness through your actions and words.

CONCLUSION

EMBRACING THE POWER OF PROPHETIC PRAYER

As we reach the end of our journey through the lives and messages of the prophets, we find ourselves enriched by their timeless wisdom and powerful lessons. Each prophet has highlighted a unique facet of our relationship with God and the transformative power of prophetic prayer. The stories of Elijah, Moses, Amos, Isaiah, Jeremiah, Ezekiel, Daniel, Hosea, Jonah, and Malachi have taught us about faith, obedience, justice, hope, perseverance, renewal, wisdom, love, and faithfulness. These themes not only define their ministries but also guide us in deepening our own prayer lives.

The bold faith of Elijah challenges us to pray with confidence and expect revival and transformation in our communities. His unwavering trust in God's power, even in the face of overwhelming odds, inspires us to approach our prayer life with the same boldness and assurance. We are reminded that our prayers have the potential to bring about significant change when rooted in faith and aligned with God's will.

Moses' journey of guidance and deliverance emphasizes the importance of seeking God's direction and trusting His promises. As we navigate the complexities of life, Moses' story encourages us to call upon God for guidance, knowing that He is our deliverer who leads us through challenges and into freedom. Our prayers should reflect our dependence on God's wisdom and our trust in His plan for our lives.

Amos' call for justice and righteousness reminds us of our responsibility to speak out against injustice and to live with integrity and humility. His message encourages us to align our prayers with God's heart for justice, interceding for those who are oppressed and marginalized. By doing so, we become instruments of God's justice and mercy in the world.

Isaiah's vision of hope and redemption invites us to maintain hope in God's promises, especially in difficult times. His prophecies assure us that God's plan includes restoration and renewal, even when we face challenges. Isaiah's message encourages us to pray for vision and hope, trusting that God's promises are steadfast and true.

Jeremiah's perseverance through trials teaches us the value of enduring faith. His unwavering commitment to God's call, despite immense challenges, inspires us to pray for strength and resilience. Jeremiah's life shows us that perseverance in prayer leads to restoration and fulfillment of God's promises.

Ezekiel's visions of renewal and rebirth highlight the transformative power of God's Spirit. His messages call us to embrace spiritual renewal and to pray for a fresh outpouring of God's Spirit in our lives and communities. Ezekiel's story encourages us to seek God's renewal, trusting that He can bring life to even the driest and most desolate places in our hearts.

Daniel's wisdom and protection in exile demonstrate the importance of seeking divine wisdom and trusting in God's protection. His life encourages us to pray for discernment and safety, knowing that God is our ultimate source of wisdom and security. Daniel's example teaches us to live with confidence in God's guidance and protection.

Hosea's story of love and redemption profoundly illustrates God's relentless love for us. His life calls us to embrace God's love and to extend it to others, praying for healing and restoration in our relationships. Hosea's message reminds us that God's love is transformative, bringing redemption and renewal to our lives.

Jonah's journey of obedience and mercy highlights the importance of responding to God's call and extending

His mercy to others. His story encourages us to pray for a heart of obedience and compassion, willing to follow God's lead and show mercy to those in need. Jonah's life teaches us that God's mercy knows no bounds and that our obedience can lead to transformation and salvation for others.

Malachi's call to faithfulness and covenant reminds us of the importance of honoring our relationship with God. His messages encourage us to remain faithful in our worship, relationships, and stewardship of resources. Malachi's story calls us to live in a way that reflects our covenant commitment to God, praying for faithfulness and integrity in all aspects of our lives.

As we integrate these principles into our prayer lives, we will experience the power of prophetic prayer. We will draw closer to God, align our hearts with His, and become instruments of His love and justice in the world. May the stories and lessons of the prophets inspire and empower us to live out our faith with boldness, integrity, and compassion. Let us continue to seek God's presence, pray with fervor, and trust in His promises, knowing that He is faithful to complete the work He has begun in us.

PRAY PROPHETICALLY EVEN THOUGH YOU MAY BE UNKNOWN

We often hear the stories of well-known prophets and leaders whose names have become synonymous with faith and courage. However, the Bible also highlights many lesser-known figures whose faithfulness and prophetic prayers had a significant impact. These "unknown" prophets remind us that God's call to prophetic prayer is not limited to the famous or the prominent; it extends to every believer, regardless of their status or recognition.

You might feel like an "unknown" in the grand scheme of things—someone whose prayers and actions seem insignificant in the vastness of the world. But take heart in knowing that God sees you, and your prayers hold immense value in His kingdom. The story of the unnamed prophet in 2 Chronicles 20, who delivered a crucial message to King Jehoshaphat, is a powerful reminder that God uses everyone who is willing to listen and obey, no matter how hidden they may seem.

Prophetic prayer is not about having a platform or a title; it is about being attuned to God's voice and being willing to speak and act on His behalf. It is about seeking God's guidance with a heart full of faith, interceding for others, and being a conduit of His will on earth. When you pray prophetically, you align yourself with

God's heart and purposes, becoming an instrument through which His power and presence can flow.

Consider the example of Gideon, who was an ordinary man called by God to deliver Israel from the Midianites. When the Israelites cried out to the Lord, God sent a prophet to remind them of His past deliverances and their need for repentance. Following this prophetic message, God called Gideon to lead a small army to victory. Gideon's story illustrates that God often chooses the unlikely and the humble to carry out His extraordinary plans.

Your prayers, though they may seem small or unnoticed, can bring about profound change. By praying prophetically, you participate in God's work of redemption and restoration. You become a beacon of His light in a world that desperately needs hope and direction. Your faithfulness in prayer can bring healing, guidance, and breakthrough in ways you might never fully see or understand.

Remember, God's power is made perfect in weakness, and His Spirit equips and empowers those who are willing to be used by Him. Your willingness to pray prophetically, even in obscurity, is a testament to your trust in God's sovereignty and His ability to use every willing heart for His glory.

So, be encouraged to step into the role of a prophetic intercessor. Seek God earnestly, listen to His voice, and pray with boldness and faith. Trust that your prayers are heard, valued, and used by God to accomplish His purposes. Whether known or unknown, your prophetic prayers are a vital part of God's unfolding story.

Mary Donna Hankla

www.ingramcontent.com/pod-product-compliance
Lightning Source LLC
Chambersburg PA
CBHW060503130626
46553CB00002B/394